Mary Queen of Scots i

C. A. Campbell

Alpha Editions

This edition published in 2022

ISBN : 9789356908758

Design and Setting By
Alpha Editions
www.alphaedis.com
Email - info@alphaedis.com

Contents

CHAPTER I.

THE SCOTLAND OF MARY'S BIRTH.

No tale of romance possesses a more lasting charm than does the simple history of Mary Stewart, Queen of Scots. Since the day on which Sir Ralph Sadler, Ambassador of Queen Elizabeth, was privileged to see her in the nursery at Linlithgow, and pronounced her a "right fair and goodly child," every fresh contribution to her history has been welcomed with unparalleled eagerness. Nor is there any indication that her life-story will lose its fascination with the lapse of time. Scarcely a year passes away that does not see a considerable addition made to the already ponderous store of Mary-Stewart literature. Nevertheless, very many even of her admirers have, to say the least, an inadequate knowledge of her life. They know her only as a heroine of romance, or as a pious widow, kneeling in devotion with the Rosary hanging at her girdle, or as a cheerful martyr resigning her head to the block; and they forget that for seven years she reigned over the most turbulent nation of Europe, that she opened and closed parliament, deliberated in the Council Chamber, led armies to the field, that, in a word, she lived a most real and stirring life.

I confess it is no easy task to present a complete and, at the same time, correct picture of her career. The difficulty is owing to the large amount of matter, written in different and contradictory spirits, with which some of the most important events of her life have been obscured. Religion, politics, patriotism, avarice, personal friendships and hatreds, either conjointly or individually, determined the actions of those who had part in framing the history of the period. It becomes necessary, therefore, to learn how far the men on whose testimony, or from whose conduct, we have to pass judgment on certain incidents in Mary's life, were influenced by one or other of these motives.

Mary Queen of Scots was born in Linlithgow Palace, in Scotland, on the 8th of December, 1542. The condition of Scotland at the time was sad and evil-boding. Her father, the well-beloved James V., was at Falkland, dying of a broken heart, in consequence of the humiliating conduct of the disaffected Scottish nobles at Solway Moss. When told that a daughter had been born to him at Linlithgow, he gave no sign of pleasure, but sadly said, "God's will be done." Then, his memory reverting to the person through whom the Stewarts had ascended the throne of Scotland, he added, "It (the crown) came with a lass and it will go with a lass." He died shortly after, in the thirty-first year of his age, leaving to his distracted country an infant queen, only six days old.

The care of the young queen devolved on her mother, Mary of Lorraine, a lady of the famous French house of Guise. Did the scope of the present sketch but sanction the digression, I should be pleased to dwell a little on the character of this distinguished woman, whose memory some historians have, according to their custom, endeavoured to blacken, but who stands out in the judgment of the best historians of every creed as a generous, forgiving and heroic woman, who conscientiously defended the rights of her daughter and maintained the laws of Scotland, until an edifying and pathetic death withdrew her from the troubled scenes in which the years of her widowhood had been passed.

It is the privilege, or perhaps the misfortune, of rulers, that their marriage is one of the first things that engage the attention of their people; and while the nursery was disturbed by the cries of the infant queen, the councils of England and Scotland were agitated with the question of her marriage. Henry VIII., of England, had an infant son, Edward, afterwards Edward VI., for whom he wished to secure from the Scottish parliament a solemn promise of marriage with the young Queen of Scots. As might be presumed, it was not so much the desire of cultivating the friendship of his northern neighbours that actuated the English monarch, as the hope of accomplishing, by means of a marriage, what his predecessors had failed to accomplish by means of the sword, the subjugation of the Scottish kingdom. To have a clear conception of the political relations between the two countries, and to understand the foundation of the English claims, it will be necessary to take a retrospective glance at the history of Scotland.

In 844, the Scots of Dalriada and various Pictish races became united under King Kenneth McAlpine. During the reign of Malcolm I., who ascended the throne of Alban a hundred years later, the district of Cumberland was, by Edmund of England, made over to the King of Scotland, on condition that the latter should, in return, render him certain assistance in time of war. The acquisition of other districts fronting the Scottish border was subsequently made, in return for offered assistance against the common enemy--the Danes. But the annexation of Cumberland was the principal source of the endless conflicts between the sister kingdoms, until the union of the crowns under James VI. For those possessions which he had acquired within the kingdom of England, the Scottish king was obliged to pay homage to his neighbouring monarch. In the course of time, however, the English Kings began to claim that the homage they received from Scotland was for the entire Scottish kingdom, as well as for the Scottish possessions within the English borders. This the Scots denied, protesting that, while paying homage for the English border lands which they had acquired, they were a free and independent people. Such a state of affairs may seem strange to us, but it was nothing uncommon in those feudal times. William the Conqueror, for instance, although independent sovereign of England, paid homage to the King of France for the dukedom of Normandy, which he held within French territory.

In those circumstances, any English king who might desire to make war against Scotland could always put forward the old claim as a plea for his action. Unfortunately, the Scottish parliament, in order to secure the release of their King, William the Lion, on one occasion acknowledged the English claim of suzerainty. A few years later, however, Richard the Lion-hearted renounced the English claim, on payment by Scotland of a certain sum of money, which that chivalrous crusader needed to defray the expenses of his expedition to the Holy Land. The country remained independent for about one hundred years; then disputes concerning the rightful successor to Alexander III. having disunited and weakened the Scottish people, Edward I. found the time opportune for renewing the old claim. Twelve competitors for the throne appeared in the field, who, being not altogether averse to sacrificing national honour to personal advantage, were willing to acknowledge the supremacy of England, in order to win the invaluable influence of Edward for their respective causes. The principal claimants were Robert Bruce--not the great Bruce--and John Baliol. Edward decided in favour of Baliol, who forthwith ascended the throne as vassal of England. But the Scottish lion was soon aroused by the encroachments of Edward, and Baliol was forced to disclaim allegiance to his patron. Entering into a league with France, he began to prepare for the invasion of England. (This was the beginning of the long-continued friendship between Scotland and France, which completely died out only with the death of the Stewart cause.) But Scotland was not prepared to cope with the haughty Longshanks, and it was reduced to the condition of a province of England. This could not endure long. Disunion, and not lack of national valour, had opened the way to defeat. A leader only was needed, and a leader soon arose in the person of William Wallace, the soldier and hero-patriot. Although Wallace, after having driven the English out of his country, did not succeed in establishing her independence on a lasting basis, nevertheless his achievements were not vain; he had aroused his countrymen to action, and his patriotic conduct before the English judges in Westminster Hall, could not fail to open the eyes of certain Scottish nobles who, from motives of self-interest, had accepted the foreign rule, to a realization of their dishonourable position. When accused of being a traitor to King Edward, Wallace replied: "I could not be a traitor to Edward, for I was never his subject."

Scarcely had death struck the torch of patriotism from the hand of Wallace, when it was caught up by a worthy successor, who had learned bravery by the side of Wallace himself. Robert Bruce was the person whom Providence had destined, not merely to defeat the enemies of his country on the field of battle, but also to unite and consolidate his kingdom and to cause it to be once more recognized as free and independent. David II., son and successor of the great liberator, died without issue, and thus the male line of the Bruce family became extinct. But the nation, being strongly attached to the memory of their deliverer, called to the throne his descendant through the female line. Bruce's daughter, Marjory, had married the Lord High Steward of Scotland, and had a son, Robert. Marjory Bruce was the "lass" to whom James V. made reference on his death-bed; and her son, who in 1370 ascended the throne as Robert II., was the first of that long, celebrated, and unfortunate line of Stewart monarchs. Brave, witty, rash, affable, obstinate, magnanimous, they exhibit a character in which all the qualities that make men beloved, and nearly all that make men great, are perversely blended with many frailties and follies. Besides, some remorseless genius would seem to have presided over their lives and to have ingeniously contrived to make their miseries greater, and their lives more pitiable, by leading them into full view of prosperity and glory before it struck them to the earth. The good Robert III. died of sorrow at the misfortune of his sons; James I., the brave, learned and wise monarch, died under the murderer's steel; James II. was killed by the bursting of a cannon; James III., thrown from his horse and wounded, was stabbed to death by an assassin; James IV., the pride and darling of the nation, fell, sword in hand, on a disastrous field of battle; James V. died of a broken heart, and that, too, like his predecessors, in the blossom of his manhood; Mary (if I be permitted to anticipate), died at the block, the victim of politico-religious utilitarianism and her cousin's jealousy; and Charles I. died at the block, the victim of a military despotism.

During these centuries successive regal minorities afforded the nobles, at all times powerful and turbulent, ample opportunity of increasing their power, until it became a standing menace to the throne. James IV., besides his other good works for the welfare of his people, did much towards reducing the power of the nobles and centralizing authority in the crown. But the progress of the country received a sudden check, and the bright career of the King was brought to a mournful close, by an event that did for Scotland, on the eve of the Reformation, what the Wars of the Roses had already done for England--deprived it of its best and bravest nobles. James' rash invasion of England ended in the doleful battle of Flodden, which robbed Scotland of her king and almost of her independence. There is, however, one feature in that sad event which is pleasing to contemplate; it was the last great battle in which a united Scotland stood with unwavering fidelity around its monarch.

By the time Mary Stewart saw the light, an unexpected element of disunion had been introduced into the national life. The religious revolution of the sixteenth century, commonly called the Reformation, had been spreading in the cities and towns of the kingdom. Already in England Henry VIII. had enriched the throne, and the greedy nobles had enriched themselves, from the spoils of churches and monasteries. By his breach with Rome, Henry had made himself an enemy to the Catholic powers, and it was important that he should strengthen his position by drawing Scotland out of its old alliance with France, and bringing it into friendship with himself. But this he could not do while Scotland remained Catholic. The title of "Defender of the Faith," which, by his rebellion against the Pope, Henry had forfeited, but which, strange to say, neither he nor his successors have ever relinquished, was conferred on James V. of Scotland in 1537. In 1540 Henry sent his wily envoy, Sir Ralph Sadler, to bring the refractory young James to his own way of thinking. Sadler came with his plan of temptation so skilfully arranged, that one would believe him fresh from the study of the fourth chapter of St. Matthew's Gospel.

First, he appealed to the vanity of the young King, representing to him that if he yielded to Henry's wishes, he would become independent of all external authority. But the device failed, and Sadler was forced to inform his master, that James continued in his persuasion that the "Bishop of Rome is the Vicar of Christ."

He next attempted to gain the Scottish King through avarice. He pointed out the wealth of the monasteries, which could be appropriated to the uses of the crown, as it had been in England. James assured him there was no need of that, for the "Kirkmen would give him all he wanted." Finally, Sadler reminded him that Henry was "stricken in years" and that by showing consideration for his uncle's wishes, James might be named his successor, and one day rule over the whole island. Yet the young northern king did not fall down and adore, but merely answered that he wished his uncle many years of life on the English throne; as for himself, he added, he was happy among his own people, and had no desire to extend his dominions.

Not all the Scottish nobles followed the example of their monarch. Across the border they could see the English nobles enriching themselves from Church property, and it was not clear to them why they should not go and do likewise. Accordingly, a number of them became remarkably industrious in the cause of the new religion, their zeal for the house of God being nowise abated by the unprecedented wealth it brought to their own house. We should greatly err, however, if we thought the avarice of the nobles of itself could have made the change of religion possible. The truth is, the state of Religion in Scotland, at that time, was not flourishing, and the country offered a good field for the growth and spread of religious innovation. The long peace from external foes which the Church had enjoyed was the occasion of a relaxation of discipline, and of a widespread indifference to the full observance of religious duties. The custom of appointing lay abbots, called Commendatory Abbots, to the charge of the temporalities of monasteries, was another evil. This office was frequently controlled by powerful lords, who had their own sons appointed thereto, not on account of their virtue or their learning, but just because they were scions of noble houses who had to be provided for. But what made the way smoothest for the "Reformers" was the ignorance of the people in matters of Christian doctrine. The wars in which the country had been for centuries engaged, had left little or no time for the cultivation of the arts of peace, except within the monasteries. Had the people been properly instructed in their religion, the work of the "Reformers" would have made but little headway in Scotland. A Reformation in the true sense--a recalling of the people, high and low, to the practice of their religious duties--was necessary; new creeds were not necessary. But the true Reformation began too late; in the meantime there came a revolution in which the religious fabric of centuries was overthrown, and a new profession of faith, gotten up in a few days by a committee of divines, was adopted by Act of Parliament. The monasteries and churches, which vied in point of richness and architectural beauty with the best on the Continent, were plundered and demolished. Voluminous libraries, containing, together with the works of the Ancients and the writings of the Church Fathers, precious manuscript histories of Scottish institutions, were made the fuel of bonfires; and the treasures of sculpture and painting, which had been accumulating for centuries, and in which men's religious hopes and fears were depicted by the Master artists of Medieval times, were hurled from their pedestals or consigned to the flames. While the frenzy lasted, the national loss was not considered. But cool heads soon began to deplore the wanton destruction which robbed the country of so many monuments, the history of which was interwoven with the history of Scottish patriots and heroic achievements. And in truth what true Scotsman, whatever his religious tenets, but deplores the demolition of such venerable piles as Melrose Abbey, Kelso, Scone? or who but would feel the noblest emotions of his nature awakened could he now approach the High Altar of Cambuskenneth's shrine, before which, when Scotland lay prostrate at the feet of the conqueror, the brave associates of Bruce knelt and vowed the deliverance of their country? But we must return to Mary.

CHAPTER II.

TROUBLES SURROUNDING HER CHILDHOOD.

On the death of James V., the Earl of Arran, head of the powerful house of Hamilton, became Governor of Scotland. Arran was weak and unreliable, and favourably affected, both in religion and politics, toward the English party. On the other hand, Cardinal David Beaton, Archbishop of St. Andrews, stood forth as the representative of Scottish independence and the French alliance; and through his influence the progress of negotiations for the English alliance was checked. But, for reasons which I need not delay to explain, an agreement of marriage between Mary and Edward was afterwards signed. So strongly, however, were the masses of the people opposed to any measure that might bring Scotland under the power of the "auld enemy," and so enraged were they at certain humiliating conditions attached to the marriage contract, that the treaty was broken up within a fortnight after it had been signed. "I assure you," said a Scotsman to the English envoy, "that our nation, being a stout nation, will never agree to have an Englishman King of Scotland; and though the whole nobility of the realm should consent to it, yet the common people, and the stones of the streets would rise and rebel against it."

Henry VIII., whose patience was not his predominant virtue, was enraged at this opposition to his will, and hastened troops into Scotland, both by land and sea, with instructions so savagely cruel, that we could hardly believe them to have been issued did we not see them realized in the subsequent conduct of the soldiery. On the 3rd of May, 1544, an English fleet suddenly appeared off Leith, which, in conjunction with a land army, proceeded to carry out the instructions of their royal master, namely, "To put all to fire and sword, to burn Edinburgh town, and to raze and deface it when you have sacked it and gotten what you can out of it, as that it may remain for ever a perpetual memory of the vengeance of God lighted upon it for their falsehood and disloyalty." "Do what you can," the instructions continue, "out of hand and without long tarrying, to beat down and overthrow the Castle, sack Holyrood House and as many towns and villages about Edinburgh as you conveniently can. Sack Leith and burn and subvert it and all the rest, putting man, woman and child to fire and sword, without exception, when any resistance shall be made against you. And this done, pass over to Fifeland and extend like extremities and destructions to all towns and villages whereunto ye may reach conveniently; not forgetting amongst all the rest to spoil and turn upside down the Cardinal's town of St. Andrews, as the upper stone may be the nether, and not one stick stand by another; sparing no creature alive within the same, especially such as either in friendship or blood be allied to the Cardinal."

Another army sent into Scotland in September of the same year, converted the southern portion of the country almost into a waste, no scruple being made of burning mothers and children in their homes. Between the 8th and the 23rd of September, the army destroyed, among other things, seven monasteries, sixteen castles, five market towns, two hundred and forty-three villages, thirteen mills and three hospitals. These barbarities had the effect of uniting the two parties in Scotland and of retarding the very movement that Henry had hoped they should accelerate.

The greatest obstacle to the progress of Henry's designs on Scotland was still Cardinal Beaton. Beaton was not only a distinguished prelate, but also a statesman of European reputation. Henry was anxious to get him out of the way; but negotiations for his murder, though entered into on various occasions, fell through, because the interested parties could not agree on the price of the Cardinal's blood. However, the work was accomplished later; on the 29th of May, 1546, a band of conspirators entered the Castle of St. Andrews, murdered the Cardinal and, having dressed his corpse in priestly vestments, suspended it from the Castle wall. Henry was shortly afterwards called to his reward, but the war against Scotland was carried on by Somerset, the Protector, and in September, 1547, Scottish independence being seriously threatened, after the disastrous battle of Pankie, the young queen was quickly removed from Sterling and hurried away to the Priory on Inchmahone, in the lake of Menteith, in Perthshire. Here, unconscious of the fierce conflicts of which she was the occasion, Mary passed her days in childish sports, in company with her four playmates, who were destined to become her maids of honor--Mary Beaton, Mary Seton, Mary Fleming and Mary Livingston.

Some decisive step with regard to the young queen had soon to be taken. The Estates convened and decided to give her in marriage to the Dauphin, and to send her to France to be educated. Accordingly, on the 7th of August, 1548, Mary, being then scarcely six years old, embarked at Dunbarton, and six days later landed at Roscoff, near Brest. Surrounded by every mark of respect corresponding to her dignity, she was conducted to the Court of Henry II., and was henceforward treated with the distinction due to a crowned queen (for the coronation ceremony had been performed in Scotland), and the betrothed of the heir to the French throne.

CHAPTER III.

THE YOUNG QUEEN OF SCOTS IN FRANCE.

Those who have been accustomed to hearing the French court of that time spoken of as dissolute and vicious, and who have furthermore taken for granted that Mary's early life was shaped by the unsavoury habits of the courtiers, and that the crimes of which she was afterwards accused were only the natural outgrowth of her early training, will do well to remember that her education was not intrusted to the French court or courtiers. Antoinette de Bourbon, maternal grandmother of the young queen, a lady eminent throughout France for her virtues, was the person in whose hands Mary of Lorraine had placed the religious education of her child. The brave Duke of Guise (who had won Calais from the English) and his brother the Cardinal, were also particularly interested in the welfare of their little niece. To these Mary, from the beginning, became warmly attached, and their landless and uninterrupted solicitude for her well-being, sealed that reciprocal love of uncles and niece which lasted until death.

Mary was already Queen of Scotland and betrothed of the future King of France, and would probably succeed to the throne of England; nothing, therefore, was overlooked that would help to qualify her for the high position to which she was destined. Her education did not stop with the lighter accomplishments suited to her sex and station; the deeper studies of literature, ancient and modern; history, Sacred Scripture, the languages and the fine arts, were assiduously attended to. An interesting document in the form of a Latin exercise book which she used when about twelve years of age, is preserved in the National Library in Paris. It contains sixty-four themes, written in clear characters, which, however, vary in appearance according to the quality of the pen and ink she happened to have at hand. She writes on subjects taken from Plato, Cicero and other classical authors; she cites different works of Erasmus; she discusses the history of certain learned women of antiquity; she speaks of the profit to be derived from the study of Holy Scripture if approached with a pure heart; and among other things she has a theme on Purgatory, thrown into the form of an epistle addressed to Calvin. Mary's physical, mental and moral development were studiously watched, and carefully reported to her mother in Scotland. When she had just completed her eleventh year, the Cardinal of Guise, in a letter to her mother, writes of her as follows: "Your daughter has grown much taller and she daily improves in goodness and virtue, in beauty and intelligence. She could not possibly make greater progress than she does in all that is excellent and of good reputation. Never have I seen her equal in this realm, either among high or low.... You may be assured that in her you have a daughter who will be the greatest of comforts to you." Further on the

Cardinal drops a remark which shows that Mary had already developed a trait of character that was conspicuous throughout the remainder of her life. "In the settlement of your daughter's establishment, it is my opinion that there should not be anything that is either superfluous or mean, for meanness is the thing which, of all others, she hates most in the world."

In a letter written to her mother on the occasion of her first communion, Mary uttered a prayer which we who know--what she could not then know--the trials that awaited her, cannot read without being touched by the sad contrast between her first bright hope and the subsequent gloom that settled over her life. "I have come," she said, "to Meudon to Madame my grandmother, in order to keep the feast of Easter, because she and my uncle--Monsieur the Cardinal--wish that I should take the Sacrament. I pray to God very humbly to give me grace that I may make a good beginning."

On Sunday, the 4th of April, 1558, the fair Scottish queen, who was now in her sixteenth year, was married to the young Dauphin, in the Cathedral of Notre Dame. All Paris was astir in its festive garments. Scotland and France vied in adding to the splendour of the feast; the choicest music swelled along the high arches of the grand old cathedral; the streets of the gay capital re-echoed with the popular demonstrations; nor need we doubt that the martial strains of the Highland pipes mingled with the livelier tones of the French fife and drum. According to a chronicler of the event, it was the universal opinion of the multitude that, "if Scotland be a possession of value, she who is queen of that realm is far more precious, for if she had neither crown nor sceptre, her single person, in her divine beauty, would be worth a kingdom."

In the following November, Mary Tudor, Queen of England, died, and Mary Stewart, at least in the opinion of the Catholics, who did not acknowledge the legitimacy of Elizabeth, daughter of Ann Boleyn, became, by right, Queen of England. Mary's title to the crown of England came through her paternal grandmother, the Princess Margaret, eldest sister of Henry VIII. A few months later, the death of the French King brought the Dauphin to the throne, and Mary became Queen of France. A little more than a year afterwards, she was left a widow of eighteen. She had all along been, and still was, the pride and admiration of France; yet she could truly say, "Now, I'm in the world alone." Her father had died when she was an infant; her father-in-law, who was strongly attached to her, had been cut off by a sudden death; her husband died shortly after; and a few months later, the news of her mother's death, under distressing circumstances, reached her. No wonder she turned her thoughts away from royal splendour and gave herself up to meditation on the hollowness of worldly greatness. No wonder it took all the influence of her friends to persuade her from entering the Convent at Rheims and passing the remainder of her days under the habit of an humble nun. But this was not permitted her; and the question of her return to Scotland began to be discussed. The Estates of Scotland convened to consider the conditions on which they would permit the return of their Sovereign. The men who led this movement had shortly before been in open rebellion, and, with the assistance of Elizabeth of England, had carried on war against the Queen-Regent, Mary of Lorraine. They had furthermore concluded a treaty with Elizabeth that was prejudicial to Mary's right of succession to the English throne; and had, by Act of Parliament, proscribed the Catholic religion in Scotland. The articles of the treaty and the acts against Catholic worship had been presented to Mary for ratification; but she had declined to sanction them, the question being weighty and she being without counsel of her nobles; more especially, however, because these were not the work of the Scottish nation, but of a faction in league with Queen Elizabeth.

Indeed, the English Ambassador to Paris, Sir Nicholas Throckmorton, had repeatedly urged Mary to ratify the treaty of Edinburgh. It was after an interview with her on this subject that this shrewd and observant agent of Elizabeth and Cecil penned for the information of the English court, the following description of the young widow, which is valuable as the testimony of an enemy who knew her well:--

"During her husband's life no great account was made of her, for that being under bond of marriage and subjection to him (who carried the burden and care of all her matters), there was offered no great occasion to know what was in her. But since her husband's death, she hath shewed (and so continueth) that she is of great wisdom for her years, and of equal modesty, and also of great judgment in the wise handling of herself and her matters; which, increasing with her years, cannot but turn greatly to her commendation, reputation, honour and great benefit to herself and her country.... Assuredly she carries herself so honourably and discreetly that one cannot but fear her progress."

Mary's "modesty and honour," therefore, were already the cause of alarm to her English foes. What wonder, then, if they strove to dispoil her of both, or that failing, endeavoured to convince her subject that she had cast them both from her?

Two delegates were sent from Scotland to negotiate with their Queen concerning her return. One represented the Congregation,[#] or what may be called the Revolutionary party--and this was Mary's own half-brother, Lord James Stewart, later known as the Earl of Moray; the other, John Leslie, afterwards Bishop of Ross and the life-long friend of Mary, represented what may be called the old loyal party. The suspicions entertained by the loyal party as to the honesty of Lord James' intentions are revealed by the fact that Leslie advised Mary to have him arrested and detained in France, until she should be firmly seated on the throne. If she did not care to do this, Leslie recommended that, instead of going direct to Edinburgh, which was the stronghold of the Congregation, she should land at Aberdeen, where the Earl of Huntly, with twenty thousand of her loyal subjects, was prepared to welcome her and conduct her in triumph to Edinburgh. And when we consider the influence of the powerful Gordon, who even then was "Cock of the North," it seems probable that the Congregation, without the aid of Elizabeth, could have raised no force sufficient to oppose him.

[#] Since December, 1557, when a certain number of Scottish nobles, at the instance of Knox, solemnly pledged themselves to support the new religion and "to forsake and renounce the congregation of Satan,"--by which they meant the Catholic Church,--the Protestants in Scotland had been known as the Congregation.

But Mary--for what reason we are not informed, but probably from her aversion to strife and bloodshed--declined the invitation of the Catholic Earl, and decided to return to Scotland under the patronage of neither the circumcised "Saints" of the Congregation, nor the uncircumcised Philistines of the Gordon country, but as a messenger of peace who would unite all parties in the bonds of mutual forbearance, and would seek her support in the undivided loyalty of the realm. So far she had won all hearts, and had met no man but would have thought it a privilege to be permitted to devote his life to her service. May we not suspect that she hoped her personal influence, which had hitherto known victory only, would soften the animosity of rebel lords and religious fanatics?

At any rate she prepared to depart for Scotland. "All the bravest and noblest gentlemen of France assembled themselves around the fairest of Queens and women," to give her a last proof of their love and respect. Among the Scottish nobles who formed part of her cortege on her way to Calais, was he who, a few years later, became the evil genius of her life--the brave and reckless Earl of Bothwell. In the following soliloquy, the unfortunate Earl, outlawed and pining away in a Danish prison, has been made to express his impressions of the young widow when he first knew her in France:--

"O Mary, Mary, even now,

Seared as I am to shame,

The blood grows thick around my heart

At utterance of thy name!

I see her as in by-gone days,

A widow, yet a child,

Within the fields of sunny France,

When heaven and fortune smiled.

*   *   *   *   *

O lovelier than the fairest flower

That ever bloomed on green,

Was she, the darling of the land,

The young and spotless queen.

The sweet, sweet smile upon her lips,

Her eyes so kind and clear,

The magic of her gentle voice,

That even now I hear!

And nobles knelt, and princes bent,

Before her as she came;

A queen by gift of nature she,

More than a queen in name."[#]

[#] "Bothwell," by William Edmondstoune Aytoun.

On the 15th of August, 1561, having bid farewell to her uncles, the Cardinal and the Duke of Guise, to her other relatives and the large number of friends and admirers who accompanied her to the water's edge, she embarked at Calais and turned with a heavy heart to her new home, where her mother, only a few months before, had been denied a grave; where the death of her husband had been made the subject of rude jibes, and where she herself had been denounced by the leader of the new religion, as another Jezebel. France may be said in the meantime to have been in mourning; and the words of the poet Ronsard, poetry though they be, express a feeling that was common to the nation.

"Ho! Scotland," he writes, "I would that thou mightest wander like Delos on the face of the sea, or sink to its profoundest depths, so that the sails of thy bright queen, vainly striving to seek her realm, might suddenly turn and bear her back to her fair Duchy of Tourraine."

Six days after her departure, having evaded, under cover of a dense fog, the English cruisers sent out to intercept her, she landed at Leith, and proceeded to the Royal Palace of Holyrood at Edinburgh.

CHAPTER IV.

FACING TROUBLES IN SCOTLAND.

The news of the unexpected arrival of the young Queen, who had come unattended by armed force, and had committed herself to the chivalry of the nation, awakened a degree of enthusiasm even in the stern "professors" of the Congregation. Feelings of loyalty to a long line of monarchs die hard in the human breast, and especially was this so in those days when the monarch, in the estimation of his people, stood for something more than the chairman of a national committee; and the mass of the Scottish people, whether adherents of the old religion, or professors of the new, saw in the fair Queen who had come amongst them the representative of a line of brave Sovereigns, around whom their forefathers had fought and died for national independence, and whose deeds of bravery were fresh in Scottish song and tradition, indeed, the influence which Mary wielded over the people was greater than could well be expected. Shortly after her arrival, a number of the most zealous nobles of the Congregation came to Edinburgh to help Knox banish the Mass from her household. But, after a few visits to Holyrood, their fierce fervour disappeared. "I have been here now for five days," remarked one of them to a friend, "and at the first I heard every man say, 'Let us hang the priest,' but after that they had been twice or thrice in the Abbey, all that fervency passed. I think there be some enchantment whereby men are bewitched." And in truth it can be said that, with scarcely an exception, no one ever came directly under the influence of Mary Stewart without being, in some degree, impressed in her favour.

But in spite of the favourable signs that were manifested on her arrival, no grave observer could contemplate her environment and fail to foresee discord, rebellion and her almost inevitable overthrow. There were the fierce nobles who, a few months before, had been in arms against her mother, and who were enjoying the property of the Church, which it was now their interest to combat. There were the stern "Professors" of the Congregation, of which Knox was the life and force, who considered her an idolatress, and, consequently--according to the Jewish criminal code, which they held in special esteem--deserving of death. There was her half-brother, Lord James, gruff, reticent and ambitious, watching for a turn of affairs that might bring him to the throne; and there, too, was Elizabeth, with her able and unscrupulous Secretary, Cecil, who had already fomented and supported rebellion in Scotland, and even now had emissaries at work for the overthrow of the young northern Queen. Worst, perhaps of all, Mary had very little counsel on which she could rely. Allowing for poetical exaggeration, a good deal of truth is contained in the words of the Jacobite bard:--

"She stood alone without a friend,

On whom her arm might lean,

No true and trusty counsellors

Were there to serve their Queen;

But moody men, with sullen looks,

And faces hard and keen."

Mary was not long in Scotland before her courage was put to the test. It had been stipulated by Lord James that she should be free to have Mass in her own house. It would seem, however, that the zealots of the Congregation had little expected that in face of their strong opposition to her religion, the young Queen would venture to practice it on her return. If so, they miscalculated the extent to which she had inherited the high spirit and unflinching courage of her bravest ancestors.

The first Sunday after her arrival, she ordered Mass to be celebrated in the Chapel-Royal of Holyrood. A party of the Congregation, headed by Patrick, Lord Lindsay, rushed into the apartment and attacked the Chaplain. The Queen immediately published a proclamation to the effect that she did not intend to interfere with the form of religion she had found established in Scotland, and that she commanded her subjects not to molest any of her servants or household. Shortly afterwards she made a tour of the country, and on her return to Edinburgh, learned that the Provost and his brethren in office had, in the meantime, issued a proclamation commanding all Papists, under penalty of death for the third offence, to depart from the town. She caused the bailies who were responsible for this act to be removed from office, and issued a counter-proclamation, permitting "All good and faithful subjects to repair to, or leave Edinburgh, according to their pleasure or convenience."

Knox was horrified at the Queen's action, and immediately predicted a sudden plague. But what annoyed him most was, that certain Protestant lords, who had professed strong opposition to the Mass, were now inclined to tolerate it in the Queen's chapel. He took care, in his weekly sermons, to make known his opinion of these "politick heads" and to give the people timely warning of the chastisement with which God would certainly visit the nation for permitting idolatry.

The young Queen, who was still in her teens, must have keenly felt the reproaches that were being cast on herself and her religion, and, although she succeeded in showing herself cheerful in company, we may be sure her heart was sad and that memory often carried her back to earlier days, in which she experienced nothing but gentle treatment and the respectful homage of a nation of brave men, ready to draw the sword in her defence. However, it would be unjust to the Scottish people to think that the treatment which Mary received in Edinburgh was a correct index to the feeling of the country at large. The hearts of the Scottish people were with their Queen, and remained with her unto the end. Her fiercest enemies were found in the extreme religious party led by Knox. An amicable understanding with these was impossible. The Protestant nobles--except those who were zealous followers of Knox--did not, as far as I can see, care much what religious devotions the Queen practised, so long as she took no steps towards restoring the old religion. The fact that many of them had enriched themselves from church property readily explains their opposition to every movement in that direction.

But the turbulent section of the nobles and the Congregation controlled by Knox, were not the people of Scotland. This is a fact it would be well to note, for, it seems to me, many people fall into the error that the friends and the enemies of Mary in Scotland were divided on purely religious lines. It is true, the storm in which she was shipwrecked, was mainly a religious one; yet all the Protestants were by no means opposed to her. Many of her best friends, who stood by her in every peril, and supported her cause until the last hope of her restoration was dead, were Protestant nobles.

Early in Mary's reign there appears to have been some discontent among certain Catholic nobles, who seemed disposed to attempt the restoration of the old faith by force of arms. The Earl of Huntly said that, if the Queen would "sanction him in it, he could set up the Mass again in the three countries." She was as zealous in the cause of religion, and willing to suffer as much for it as Huntly; but the prospect of effecting any permanent good by such means, was extremely poor. If the struggle would be left to Scotland itself, Huntly's project would be more deserving of consideration. But Queen Elizabeth would never, while she could prevent it, allow her adversaries to gain advantages in Scotland; and in the event of the Scottish Catholics attempting to gain freedom of worship for themselves her gold and her soldiers would soon flow over the border, as they did in the regency of Mary of Lorraine. But apart from this, Mary was opposed to civil strife. She had come to the country in a peaceful manner, hoping, by a peaceful policy, to conciliate the minds of her people and finally to obtain an alleviation of the ills under which her Catholic subjects were suffering. But the difficulties with which she had to contend were not fully understood by her relations in France, nor, at the outset, even by the Pope; and it is not improbable that for a while they feared she was not so industrious as she should be in promoting the interests of her religion. And to this day a number of her Protestant biographers--some of them enthusiastic vindicators of her honour--speak of her leanings towards Protestantism, either from policy or from conviction. Some say that early in her reign she, through policy, openly favoured the Protestant cause, and as proof of her favour overthrew--which she undoubtedly did--the powerful house of Gordon, head of which was the Catholic Earl of Huntly. Others think if the proper means had been employed, she would have become a Protestant from conviction, and, in support of their opinion, they adduce her readiness to read Protestant controversial works, and that state of religious doubt which, they say, she manifested in a certain conversation with Knox.

A distinguished Scottish biographer of Mary's, the late Sir John Skelton, has thought that the uncharitable treatment she received from Knox was the principal cause why she remained a Catholic. "Knox," he writes, "was the foremost of the Reformers; yet Mary had found that Knox was narrow-minded, superstitious, and fiercely intolerant,--so narrow-minded, intolerant and superstitious that he had no difficulty in believing that the orderly course of nature was interrupted because the Queen dined on wild fowl and danced till midnight. If this was Protestantism, she would have none of it. Nor can we blame her much. The eccleciastical dictator at Edinburgh was as violent and irrational (it might well appear to her) as the ecclesiastical dictator at Rome. Was it worth her while to exchange the infallible Pope of the Vatican for the infallible Pope of the High Street?"[#] (Maitland of Lethington, Vol. II., Chap. I.)

[#] The inconsistency of those who, having appealed to private judgment from the authority of the Pope, persecuted all who would not recognize their own authority, is nowhere more conspicuous than in the case of the early Scottish Reformers. By the end of the first six months of its existence, the Congregation formulated the following anathema with which to pursue rebellious subjects: "And this his sin, by virtue of our ministry we bind, and pronounce the same to be bound in heaven and earth. We further give over into the hands and power of the devil the said A.B. of the destruction of his flesh; straitly charging all that profess the Lord Jesus, to repute and to hold him accursed, and unworthy of the familiar society of Christians; declaring unto all men that such as hereafter, before his repentance, shall haunt or familiarly accompany him are partakers of his impiety, and subject to the like condemnation."

In spite of all this, I venture to say there is no historical evidence that Mary ever contemplated a change of religion. What answer does she herself give to these statements? Just before her departure from France, in conversation with Throckmorton, the English Ambassador, who was probing her mind on the question of religion, she made what may be called a formal declaration of her faith:--

"I will be plain with you; the religion which I profess I take to be the most acceptable to God, and neither do I know, nor desire to know, any other. Constancy becometh all folks well, but none better than princes, and such as rule over realms, especially in matters of religion. I have been brought up in this religion, and who might credit me in anything, if I should show myself light in this case."

Her courageous opposition to every attempt to deprive her of Mass in the Chapel-Royal of Holyrood, is well known to readers of history; and furthermore it is evident that she continued her religious devotions there as long as it was in her power to do so.

Four years after her return to Scotland, when Randolph, the Ambassador of Elizabeth, who had been sent to her on business concerning her contemplated marriage, suggested that she should change her religion and thereby gain more favor from the English Queen, Mary indignantly answered:--

"What would you that I should make merchandise of my religion! ... It cannot be so."

Her words, in reply to those who, not long before her execution, strove to prevail on her to renounce her former "follies and abominations," throw light, if that were necessary, on what her religious convictions had all along been.

To Lord Buckhurst, who had informed her that sentence of death had been passed upon her, and had urged her to accept the spiritual ministration of the Anglican Bishop of Peterborough, she said:--

"I have never had the intention of changing my religion for any earthly kingdom, or grandeur, or good, whatever, or of denying Jesus Christ, or his name, nor will I now."

And again, the day before her execution, in answer to similar demands, she said, amongst other things:--

"I have not only heard, or read, the words of the most learned men of the Catholic religion, but also of the Protestant religion. I have spoken with them and have heard them preach, but I have been unable to find anything in them that could turn me from my first belief."

So much for Mary's own evidence. It is, to say the least, faulty reasoning, to adduce the Queen's march against the Earl of Huntly as proof that she wished, either from policy or from conviction, to support the Protestant cause. In view of the firm and unequivocal stand she had hitherto taken in defence of her religion, the presumption that she was now prepared to sacrifice its interests, is unwarranted, and, furthermore, is unnecessary, as other good and sufficient reasons for her action can readily be found.

Being young and inexperienced in dealing with such turbulent nobles as then surrounded her throne, and having extremely few persons in whom she could venture to put her trust, she at first allowed herself to be influenced in her method of government by her half-brother, the Lord James. Now, Lord James, as is commonly admitted by the best historians, hoped to work his way to the Scottish throne, despite his illegitimacy, and naturally he was anxious to overthrow every power that would prove an obstacle to the advancement of his cause. Besides, he had his eye fixed on the Earldom of Moray, which had for some time been controlled by Huntly. The obstacle could be removed, and the Earldom gained, if Huntley could be "worried" into war, and then overthrown by the authority of the Queen. Three most significant things are certain,--that Lord James acquired the Earldom of Moray (hence his title of Earl of Moray) immediately that Huntly and his house were ruined; that he attempted, without Mary's knowledge, to procure the execution of Huntly's son, George, whose life had been spared, but who had been placed in ward at Stirling; and that the Gordons never after acted towards the Queen as if they held her responsible for the injuries they had suffered, but, on the contrary, gave ample proof that they considered Moray the responsible party. However, if Mary thought no danger threatened her from the Gordon country, she could not be excused for allowing herself to be made the instrument of Lord James' ambition in so grave a matter.

The fact is, the unfortunate tragedy was the result of an old and bitter enmity between Huntly and the Lord James. The hated enemy came, confident in the support of royal authority, which he almost fully controlled, and committed acts that exasperated the proud Highland Earl, and drove him into rebellion--for to oppose Lord James in these circumstances was to resist the Queen. As far as Mary was concerned, religion had as little to do with the overthrow of the Gordons as it had to do with the execution of Chastellar.

Her conversation with Knox in which she is said to have revealed a state of religious doubt, is, to my mind, a proof of her polemical cleverness. She takes Knox on his own principle of private judgment and delicately shows him that it cannot satisfy her mind--that it cannot raise her above doubt. Knox tells her one thing; her uncle, the Cardinal, tells her another; whom is she to believe? She was setting a snare for Knox, which he could not escape, except by acknowledging an authority in religion that rested on a sounder foundation than either his or the Cardinal's opinion.

But why, it may be asked, did she not make her religious zeal more evident at the outset, by sending Bishops to the Council of Trent, in compliance with the request of the Pope, and by using her influence to obtain at least religious toleration for her Catholic subjects? The answer is simple,--because it was beyond her power to do either. She had as much as she could do to save the life of her chaplain when he said Mass in the Chapel-Royal; how could she take any steps publicly to relieve her Catholic subjects?

The report of the Papal Nuncio, Nicholas Goudanus, who came to Edinburgh in June, 1562, throws light on the helpless condition of the Queen, and disposes us to sympathize with her in the miseries she was destined to suffer at so early an age, rather than to nourish suspicions of her sincerity and good conscience. He says he was in Edinburgh a month before he could see the Queen, and even then he had to be received in private, while the members of the court were out. Of all the Bishops, the Bishop of Dunkeld alone ventured to receive him. The nuncio came to the Bishop's house disguised as a banker's clerk, and, according to a pre-arranged device to avert suspicion, the conversation during dinner was limited to money matters.

Mary informed the nuncio that, in order to preserve some remains of the Catholic faith, she had been obliged to do many things much against her will. As regards the power exercised over her by the nobles, Goudanus remarks: "The men in power acknowledge the Queen's title, but prevent her from exercising any of the rights of sovereignty;[#] whenever her opinion does not agree with theirs, they oppose her at once. Not only that, but they deceive her as well, and frighten her with threats of an English invasion, especially when she is meditating any steps in support of her faith."

[#] This statement, however, is too sweeping.

As time advanced, Mary became more and more beloved by her people, although the opposition to her religion never abated. When, in 1563, she attended the opening of her first parliament, she was enthusiastically hailed by the populace, whose applause grew all the louder when they heard her address the assembly, not, as they had expected she would, in a strange language, but in their own native tongue, marked though it was by a foreign accent. Knox, who feared the "politick heads" among the children of God might so far fall from grace as to extend a degree of toleration to the outcast children of men, was irritated by this display of affection for the Queen, and he took revenge by denouncing the womanly vanity displayed by her and her ladies, especially the "targetting of their tails"--whatever that meant.

We are, as a rule, so much occupied with the romantic and tragic features of Mary's life, that we are apt to overlook her qualities as a ruler and the works which she accomplished for the benefit of her people. It may in brief be said, that she was deeply interested in every measure that could promote their welfare, that during her reign the country was comparatively peaceful and prosperous, and that the beneficent influence of her government is attested by various public records. Sir Thomas Craig, one of her Privy Councillors, has witnessed to her sound judgment in these words: "I have often heard the most serene Princess Mary Queen of Scotland discourse so appositely and rationally in all affairs which were brought before the Privy Council that she was admired by all.... She had not studied law; and yet, by the natural light of her judgment, when she reasoned on matters of equity and justice, she oftimes had the advantage of the ablest lawyer. Her other discourses and actions were suitable to her great judgment. No word ever dropped from her mouth that was not exactly weighed and pondered. *As for her liberality and other virtues they are well known.*"

CHAPTER V.

THE QUEEN'S MARRIAGE AND FRESH TROUBLES.

It is hardly necessary to mention that Mary--a Queen renowned throughout Europe for her beauty and accomplishments--was a prize for which the royal bachelors of the Continent eagerly grappled; and that in Scotland she was a rock upon which hopeless victims of her charms made shipwreck of their lives. Under the spell of those charms, a cool-brained Scotsman, the young Earl of Arran, went mad; and (what perhaps, should not surprise us so much), the hot-brained French poet, Chastellar, not only went mad, but was precipitated into acts of indiscretion that brought him to the scaffold. In the question of the Scottish Queen's marriage, however, Elizabeth wished to have a controlling voice, and she left the young Queen under the impression that, if she married the person of Elizabeth's own choice, her right of succession to the throne of England, in case the English Queen died without issue, would be declared. Accordingly, Elizabeth began proposing Robert Dudley, afterwards Earl of Leicester, as her choice of husband for the Queen of Scots. Leicester was a man of extremely doubtful reputation, and most likely would never be accepted by Mary, so long as she was free to reject him. He was the recognized favourite of Elizabeth, as well--a fact that makes it hard to understand why she put him forward in this connection. But, all the circumstances considered, it seems most likely that Elizabeth never expected Mary to marry Leicester. Indeed, she would rather see Mary remain unmarried; but William Maitland, the Scottish Queen's able Secretary, had been urging on Cecil the necessity of settling differences between the two Queens, and of recognizing the Scottish right of succession. Cecil made fair or evasive promises. In the meantime Elizabeth and he played the Leicester farce, to kill time, and probably in the hope that Mary, with her Stewart impulsiveness, would make some sarcastic remark on Elizabeth's policy, or that some other event would transpire upon which they might seize, as a plea for discontinuing negotiations, and as a screen behind which to develop their long-settled design for the overthrow of the northern Queen. But Mary became tired of Elizabeth's and Cecil's policy of evasion and delay, and feeling that it would be unbecoming her dignity as an independent sovereign, to allow herself to be played with and deceived, she resolved to break away from their snares and to marry where she would. She escaped Scylla only to be caught in Charybdis.

At the court of Elizabeth was an accomplished young lord of eighteen years, connected by blood with both the royal houses of Stewart and Tudor, whose father, although a Scottish Earl, had resided twenty years in England. This youth was Henry Stewart--Lord Darnley. The question of a marriage with Darnley had already been represented to Mary by his friends, and now she decided to entertain it. In May, 1655, after some opposition, especially on the part of Moray, Parliament gave its unanimous consent to the projected marriage, which was consequently celebrated on July 29th, and a new era opened in the life of Mary Stewart.

Immediately after the marriage, the royal pair were called upon to take the field against insurgent nobles. Moray, although he had given his consent to the proposed marriage, had subsequently declared against it, and had raised an insurrection in the country. He feared, so at least he professed, that the Queen's union with a "Papist" threatened the well-being of the "reformed" religion in Scotland. But whoever is versed in the Earl's history can discover another motive for his opposition, namely, his well-founded fear that Mary's marriage and the return of the Lennox Stewarts to Scotland would forever shut himself out from the throne. However, the marriage was completed and the insurgent lords summoned to appear at court, under pain of being considered rebels. They heeded not the summons, but prepared for war. With the assured support of Elizabeth, who likewise was offended, or pretended to be offended, at the Darnley marriage, what had they to fear? This was a critical moment for Mary. Would she try to coax the rebels into friendship by promises of pardon, and to conciliate Elizabeth by humble apologies for whatever in the late transaction might have offended her English cousin, or would she take up the gauntlet that had been thrown down, and risk the consequences of an armed encounter with the rebels? Her Secretary, Sir William Maitland, saw the danger that threatened his mistress and, in his correspondence with Cecil, strove to secure an adjustment of difficulties, by a reasonable and peaceful policy, notwithstanding the Darnley marriage. But Elizabeth and Cecil would not lose the favourable opportunity; they abandoned their attitude of obstruction and delay, and assumed one of aggression and command. Maitland could do no more. But there is a force which diplomacy cannot measure, and which cannot be applied through the ordinary medium of governmental machinery. Such is the force of a brave, resolute and inspiring character. Mary appealed to the loyalty of her people, and in a few days thousands of brave men were arrayed under her standard. The rebels, in spite of their attempts to raise the populace on their side, were never strong enough to venture an engagement with the Queen's forces; and after a few weeks they were seeking refuge where Scottish rebels of that period always found themselves secure--across the English border. The uprising served as a test of the popular feeling, and the test proved that the nation was devoted to Mary.

In an historical question like this, on which so much divergence of opinion has existed, one must be careful not lightly to dogmatize. This, however, may be said, that it is not easy to read the correspondence of that period between the English agents in Scotland and Berwick and the Secretary of State's office in London, without being driven to conclude that the subsequent rebellious movements that afflicted Scotland were directed largely from Westminster and aimed at the ultimate overthrow of Mary Queen of Scots.

The rebel nobles had suffered an inglorious defeat. Elizabeth, although she had encouraged them, now, with her habitual duplicity, to clear herself in the eyes of foreign princes, spurned them from her presence as traitors to their lawful Queen. Indeed, it requires more than ordinary mental insight to understand how Moray, if he was the conscientious and high-minded worthy that many of his friends claim him to have been--that "*vir pietate gravis*" of Buchanan--could have acted the part he did in that "scene of farce and falsehood" which Elizabeth contrived for her own justification. When he and the secularized Abbot of Kilwinning, as representatives of the discomfited rebels, approached their English patroness for consolation, she refused to give them audience, until they consented to make a solemn declaration in the presence of the French and Spanish Ambassadors, that she had given them no encouragement in their rebellion. When the humiliated Scotsmen finished their part, Elizabeth immediately added: "The treason of which you have been guilty is detestable; and as traitors, I banish you from my presence."

What was next to be done? Having given such great cause for displeasure to their Queen, the rebel nobles might well fear that the grants of property which many of them had received from her childlike lavishness, would be revoked at the first opportunity. It was necessary, therefore, that something should be done to prevent any measure of this kind and to cripple the power of the Queen. What means could be employed to this end?

Darnley, at the time of his marriage, was handsome and accomplished, but Cardinal Beaton, Mary's Ambassador at Paris, warned her, unfortunately all too late, against the match, saying that he was a "quarrelsome coxcomb." The truth of the remark was verified shortly after, when the boyish follies and profligate habits of the young King began to reveal themselves. Instead of being a comfort and support to his consort, who scarcely knew where to turn for trustworthy advice, and who had known nothing but suffering since she landed in the realm, Darnley only added fresh trials to her life. He looked for position that she could not grant him; he looked for authority that he had not judgment to exercise, and he became wrathy and troublesome when refused. Besides, he contracted the habit of drunkenness, and associated with low companions. Here, then, was a tool whom the cunning conspirators could use to work out their design.

There was in Mary's service, as Secretary, an Italian named David Rizzio, a man fairly well advanced in years, rather unprepossessing in appearance, but, according to the testimony of those who knew him well, very clever in business affairs, and of inflexible fidelity. Rizzio had so far been the faithful friend of Darnley; but the conspirators represented to the young King that the Italian had too much influence with the Queen, and was instrumental in withholding from him the authority he desired. Finally, the traitors in Scotland and the rebel lords sojourning in England, working on Darnley's ambition, entered into a league with him and signed a bond--Moray, the "*vir pietate gravis*" among the rest--by which they pledged themselves to give him the crown matrimonial, to advance his cause, to be friends of his friends and enemies of his enemies; Darnley in return promised the recall of the rebels and the security of their estates. Provisions to justify their rebellious enterprise were made in the alleged undue influence of Rizzio with the Queen, and the helpless foreigner was marked for death. A more shameful contract would be difficult to imagine. A few months earlier these men had taken up arms against their Queen, because she had decided on a marriage which (they said) was inimical to the interests of religion, and now they are signing a contract to subvert her authority and promote to unexpected power that self-same Darnley whose advancement they had risen in arms to prevent. Of course, nobody versed in the history of the movement believes that they intended to redeem their pledge. They had need of Darnley until the Queen should be disposed of. After that the mad youth could be easily cast aside, and the way to the throne would be clear for Moray. In defence of these nobles it may be answered, that they were acting in the interest of religion, which they were persuaded would be in danger as long as a Catholic monarch occupied the throne. I admit the interests of religion are preferable to the interests of a dynasty, and, if one must be sacrificed, it should be the dynasty. So far we might put ourselves in the place of the conspirators and frame a defence of their conduct. But unless we likewise admit that the end justifies the means we cannot deny the baseness and villany of this plot.

The work proceeds. Moray is notified to be within convenient distance of Edinburgh. On March 9th, 1566, about seven o'clock in the evening, while Mary is at supper with a few attendants and Rizzio, a door opening into a private stairway leading from Darnley's apartments to the Queen's, opens, and Darnley enters in an apparently friendly mood. The meaning of this unexpected entrance soon becomes evident. The evil-boding figure of Lord Ruthven, in full armour, appears in the door, his face haggard and his eyes sunken, for he has risen from a bed of sickness to direct the work of blood. A number of associates follow him. Rizzio, understanding their purpose, flees for protection behind the Queen, and cries out for justice. The Queen attempts to protect her faithful servant, but is rudely thrust aside, and the defenceless Secretary, being dragged, wounded and bleeding, to the door, is dispatched with fifty-six stabs. "Ah, poor Davit" (says Mary as she hears the dying Rizzio's groans)--"ah, poor Davit, my good and faithful servant; may the Lord have mercy on your soul!"

Three months after this tragedy James VI. was born. Considering the time and place chosen for the murder, we have good reason to suspect that harm was intended to the Queen herself, and to the future heir to the throne, as well as to Rizzio. Add to this the remarks dropped by a certain confidant of the conspirators, and suspicion gives place to conviction. Randolph, the English Ambassador, writing nearly a month before to Leicester, referred to the plot, and said that if it should take place "David shall have his throat cut within these ten days. Many things," he adds, "grievouser and worse than these are brought to my ears, yea, of things intended against her own person, which, because I think better to keep secret than to write to Mr. Secretary (Cecil), I speak of them but now to Your Lordship."

Mary was kept closely guarded, and Darnley himself, observing the movements of the traitors, began to fear for his own safety.

Darnley could be led by ambition into a rash act, but he had not reached that depth of wickedness in which the heart becomes callous to the feelings of humanity.

Stricken partly by remorse for his unfaithful and ungrateful conduct to his wife, and partly by fear of his threatened ruin, in the gray of the morning succeeding the night of murder, while all was still in Holyrood, the wretched and repentant youth stole quietly up to the Queen's chamber, and, throwing himself on his knees before her, said: "Ah, my Mary, I am bound to confess at this time, though now it is too late, that I have failed in my duty towards you. The only atonement which I can make for this, is to acknowledge my fault and sue for pardon, by pleading my youth and great indiscretion. I have been most miserably deluded and deceived by the persuasions of these wicked traitors, who have led me to confirm and support all their plots against you, myself, and all our family. I see it all now, and I see clearly that they aim at our ruin. I take God to witness that I never could have thought, nor expected, that they would have gone to such lengths. I confess that ambition has blinded me. But since the grace of God has stopped me from going further, and has led me to repent before it is too late, as I hope, I ask you, my Mary, to have pity on me, have pity on our child, have pity on yourself. Unless you take some means to prevent it, we are all ruined, and that speedily."

This report of Darnley's prayer for pardon is taken from a fragmentary sketch of Mary's life, written most probably by Claude Nau, her Secretary during the most part of her imprisonment in England, who, during the long hours of conversation with his captive mistress, had special opportunities of hearing her own account of that painful ordeal through which she had passed. It is all the more interesting, therefore, to note the answer that Nau attributes to the Queen. "The Queen," he continues, "still troubled with the agitation and weakness arising from the emotions of the previous night, answered him frankly, for she had never been trained to dissemble, nor was it her custom to do so: 'Sire,' she said, 'within the last twenty-four hours you have done me such a wrong that neither the recollection of our early friendship, nor all the hopes you can give me of the future, can ever make me forget it. As I do not wish to hide from you the impression which it has made on me, I may tell you that I think you will never be able to undo what you have done. You have committed a very grave error. What did you hope to possess in safety without me? You are aware that, contrary to the advice of those very persons whom you now court, I have made earnest suit to obtain for you of them the very thing which you think you can obtain through their means and wicked devices. I have been more careful about your elevation than you yourself have been. Have I ever refused you anything that was reasonable, and which was for your advantage, by placing you above those persons who to-day are trying to get both you and me into their power, that they may tread us under their feet? Examine your conscience, Sire, and see the blot of ingratitude with which you have stained it. You say you are sorry for what you have done, and this gives me some comfort; yet I cannot but think that you are driven to it rather by necessity than led by any sentiment of true and sincere affection. Had I offended you as deeply as can be imagined, you could not have discovered how to avenge yourself on me with greater disgrace and cruelty. I thank God that neither you nor anyone in the world can charge me with ever having done or said aught justly to displease you, were it not for your own personal good. Your life is dear to me, and God and my duty oblige me to be as careful of it as of my own. But since you have placed us both on the brink of the precipice, you must now deliberate how we shall escape the peril.'"

Such we can well believe to have been the feeling words of the outraged wife and queen. She had been humiliated by her husband in the eyes of the nation and of the world; and the ingratitude of him to whom she had been so devoted had inflicted on her heart a wound that she feared time could never heal. The bonds of love, which had been severed in spite of her and could not be reunited by an act of her will, no longer bound her to him, but "God and her duty" did, and his life would still be dear to her.

A plan of escape was arranged, and Darnley, acting with more coolness and shrewdness than was his wont, had the guards removed from the royal apartments, and, two nights later, he and Mary, accompanied by a few faithful attendants, having stealthily escaped from the palace by a back way, mounted their horses and hurried off to Dunbar.

Once more free to appeal to the loyalty of her people, the Queen had nothing to fear. The traitor lords, outwitted and alarmed, dispersed and fled, some-- especially those most prominent in the execution of the murder--betaking themselves across the border, and others withdrawing to retreats in the country. Mary was now in a position in which, had she been of a vindictive nature, she could have taken complete revenge on her enemies. But her habitual clemency prevailed, and her ear was soon again open to the prayers for pardon that reached her from the conspirators.

Her generous conduct could not fail to win hearts even among her former foes, and when, three months afterwards, James VI. was born in Edinburgh Castle, hearty demonstrations of joy marked the event throughout the whole realm. "I never," wrote the French Ambassador, Le Croc, to Cardinal Beaton, "saw Her Majesty so much beloved, honoured and esteemed, nor so great a harmony among all her subjects as at present is by her wise conduct; for I cannot perceive the smallest difference or division."

But the seeds of dissension were still alive. A new Cabinet had been formed in which hitherto discordant elements were mechanically united. Atholl, Huntly and Bothwell held prominent places; and Moray, who, by a plausible story, had exonerated himself from responsibility in the Rizzio murder, was taken into confidence. Maitland was afterwards admitted to his former post of Secretary. Darnley was furious against Moray and Maitland; against Bothwell he had no complaint, a circumstance worth noting. He was displeased with Mary because she allowed herself to be influenced by Moray and Maitland, whom he believed to be traitors. There may, perhaps, be some justification for the unfortunate Darnley's conduct at this juncture. It is possible that his brief complicity with the late conspirators had taught him a lesson which Mary, who was clement and forgiving almost to a fault, had yet to learn, namely, the deep treachery of some in whom she was putting her trust. Be this as it may, Darnley soon began to reap the bitter fruits of his mad crime. The nobles that he had left in the lurch cordially hated him; the Queen, whom he had so grievously betrayed, while she did what she could to please and pacify him, could not entrust him with the power he desired. He became the source of keen and uninterrupted grief to Mary, which added to her partial loss of health since the birth of her son, and the political dangers that threatened her independence, made her wish for death. She was brought to the point of death by an illness with which she was stricken during a visit to the remote border hamlet of Jedburgh, in October, 1566, but recovered to drag on her weary life. Her health and spirits, however, seem to have been considerably broken. "The Queen breaketh much," wrote Drury, "and is subject to frequent fainting fits." Melville, her close acquaintance, says, "she was somewhat sad when solitary." The French Ambassador gives his opinion as to the cause of her troubles: "I do believe the principal part of her disease to consist of a deep grief and sorrow, nor does it seem possible to make her forget the same. Still she repeats these words: 'I could wish to be dead.'"

The touch of care had blanched her cheek, her smile was sadder now;
The weight of royalty had pressed too heavy on her brow.

CHAPTER VI.

THE TRAGEDY OF KIRK O'FIELD AND ITS SEQUEL.

Darnley left the court in one of his sullen moods in December, 1566, and shortly after was stricken with smallpox at Glasgow. Notwithstanding his past ingratitude and infidelity, Mary, on hearing of his misfortune, sent her own physician to attend him, and a little later, having proceeded to Glasgow herself, brought him back with her to Edinburgh. Not yet being free from infection, he was placed in a house known as the Kirk O'Field, on the outskirts of the city. Mary visited him frequently and, as far as could be judged from outward signs, a complete reconciliation was effected. But the evil genius of the Stewarts again held sway. On February 10th, about 3 o'clock in the morning, the Kirk O'Field was blown into the air with gunpowder, and the mortal career of Darnley, who had just turned his twentieth year, was brought to a tragic close. Suspicions pointed to Bothwell as the author of the crime. The Earl of Lennox, Darnley's father, sued for a trial. Bothwell promptly offered himself up, and, being tried before his peers, was acquitted.

I have now arrived at the most complicated question in Mary's history, and before offering an opinion on the events that ensued, I shall mention some of them in chronological order.

Bothwell was acquitted on April 12th; on April 24th, Mary, while returning from a visit to her child at Stirling, was intercepted by him, and--willingly or unwillingly--carried off to the Castle of Dunbar. Twelve days afterwards, a promise of marriage having first been obtained from her, she was brought back to Edinburgh by Bothwell and lodged in the Castle. Eight days later she was married to Bothwell in Holyrood, before a Protestant minister.

These events have all along been interpreted in two widely different senses. One interpretation makes Mary an accomplice in the murder of her husband; the other makes her an innocent but injured woman. The historians hostile to her, catching their inspiration from the pages of George Buchanan, maintain that previously to Darnley's murder, she was familiar beyond due measure with Bothwell; that when she visited Darnley at Glasgow, it was as the agent of Bothwell to enveigle the intended victim to where he could be conveniently dispatched; that the reconciliation was feigned on her part; that when the murder was accomplished, she used her authority to shield Bothwell; and, finally, that she was carried off by him according to her own desire.

I admit that from a slight study of her life one is apt to be impressed with the thought, that the Mary Stewart of this period is not the Mary Stewart of earlier, or even later times. Something unusually weak, which leaves the suspicion of guilt, seems to characterize her conduct. I believe, however, that the more fully the sources of information are studied, the clearer will it appear that no evidence on which she can be justly convicted, has yet been adduced; but that, on the contrary, the conviction will grow in the minds of sincere enquirers, that she was first gravely injured, and next gravely calumniated, for party ends. It should be borne in mind that an accused person must be presumed innocent until his guilt is proved. This is a principle recognized in all law, and one that has something exceptionally strong to recommend it in the present case.

Until the death of Darnley, no word had been uttered against Mary's character as a woman. On the contrary, her praises were sounded on all sides, and even those who were leagued with her foes sometimes bore testimony to her virtues. The Privy Council itself, shortly before Darnley fell ill, spoke of him as one "honoured and blessed with a good and virtuous wife." But when lying served the purpose, especially in a struggle against a Papist "idolatress," who would scruple at it? Men who could unctuously quote Scripture, while engaged in the most disgraceful and unlawful work, and could, as Skelton thinks, perjure themselves with a good conscience, could hardly be expected to lose an opportunity of blackening the character of an unsanctified woman, for the glory of God and the advancement of Calvinism.

Who, on the other hand, were Mary's accusers? They were those who profited by her overthrow; those who had been known traitors and had been guilty of grievous offences against her; and those who, beyond doubt, have been convicted of calumniating her in many particulars. Of the last mentioned class the most notorious is George Buchanan, a man who owed his life to her clemency, who had been enriched by her warm-hearted liberality, who had penned his most polished verses in praise of her distinguished beauty and virtues, but who, when misfortune fell upon her, sold his venal pen to her enemies, and clothed in classical Latin the calumnies by which they hoped to overthrow her cause and establish their own. Now, students of this period of Scottish history know that Buchanan has been convicted of calumny in many particulars of Mary's life. This is beyond controversy, established by official records of the time. The presumption of calumny, therefore, attaches to his other accusations, and until these are proved to be true from reliable sources, they cannot decide anything against her. Furthermore, Buchanan's "Detectio," which was written to ruin Mary's cause in England, was prepared at the instigation of her enemies, and Buchanan's services were engaged only because he was a good Latinist. "The book was written by him," writes Cecil, "not as of himself, nor in his own name, but according to the instructions given him by common conference of the Lords of the Privy Council of Scotland"--the Moray party. It may also be mentioned that while the English translation of the "Detectio" was fathered by Cecil, and dedicated to Queen Elizabeth, the "Defence" of Mary, written by Bishop Leslie, was suppressed by the authorities at Westminster immediately it appeared.

So much for presumptive argument; but how explain the strange series of events after Darnley's murder?

Mary, after the murder of her husband, was like one who does not know what moment a mine is going to explode under her feet. She had got an inkling, through reports from London, gathered by her Ambassador in Paris, of the plot to murder Rizzio, of the conspiracy against the life of Darnley, and of harm intended to herself. The two first having been so emphatically verified, had she not reason to fear that the next would soon be consummated in her own person? Her support, too, if we except Bothwell, was, at that critical time, slender indeed. Moray, her Prime Minister who, with something akin to the wild goose instinct of approaching storms, always managed to get away whenever any disagreeable work was ready for execution, had left Edinburgh on the eve of the murder and remained absent.

It is commonly asserted by Mary's adversaries that Bothwell's trial was a farce; nor do I deny that it was. But was Mary responsible for the farce any more than Bothwell's peers who acquitted him? One reason why the trial proved a farce was, that Bothwell had too many secrets in his keeping-- secrets which, others besides himself, who perhaps were uttering expressions of pious horror at the crime, were about as deeply stained with the blood of Darnley as he. I do not claim that the Queen was perfectly persuaded of Bothwell's innocence. I say, however, that as matters then stood, there were various reasons that well might lead her to believe a plot had been formed against him; some of which were, on the one hand, the treasonable character of many who were now opposed to him, and, on the other, Bothwell's strict loyalty. With regard to this celebrated Earl, it may, I think, be truly said, that whatever his faults or his vices, besides being the most powerful, he had proved himself one of the most loyal of the Scottish nobles. James Hepburn (Earl of Bothwell) had inherited many important offices. He was Lord Admiral of Scotland, Keeper of Edinburgh Castle and of Hermitage Castle, Sheriff of the Western Lothians, and Lieutenant of the Border. No Scottish nobleman of his rank was more sincerely hated by Elizabeth. As early as 1560, Throckmorton, the English Ambassador to Paris, referred to the "glorious, boastful, rash and hazardous" Bothwell as one who should be watched. The sword of Bothwell was never wanting when the cause of his sovereign required its aid. A Protestant in religion, he had stood by Mary of Lorraine in her troubles with the Anglicizing party, and had intercepted a quantity of Elizabeth's gold that had been sent to the Scottish rebels; he had supported Mary herself against the Moray faction who revolted after her marriage with Darnley; and he was one of the first to escape from Holyrood on the night of Rizzio's murder, and arouse the country in her defence. In view of these facts, and of the widespread treachery existing among the nobles, nobody should be surprised if, at the time of the Kirk O'Field tragedy, Bothwell, considered in his public character, stood high in the opinion of the Queen and was regarded as her strongest and surest defence against the dangers by which she was encompassed.

A week after Bothwell's acquittal, a curious deed was accomplished which helps to explain the events that immediately followed. All the influential members except one, who were present at the Parliament held the same day, signed a document known in history as the "Ainslie Tavern Band," by which they engaged to do all in their power to promote a marriage between Bothwell and the Queen. In addition to this, if we accept the testimony of Claude Nau, these nobles sent a deputation to Mary, who represented that, seeing the disturbed condition of the realm, it was necessary that she should marry, and unanimously pressed her to accept Bothwell for husband. Mary refused, and reminded them of the report current about his connection with her late husband's death. The deputies had a ready reply. Bothwell, they said, had been legally acquitted by the Council; besides (to quote Nau), "they who made the request to her do so for the public good of the realm, and as they were the highest of the nobility, it would be for them to vindicate a marriage brought about by their advice and authority."

It is difficult to discover the motives that prompted some of the nobles to sign this objectionable bond. In this, very probably, as in many similar instances, indifferentism, self-interest, or fear of differing from the stronger party, led a number to subscribe. But, if we read the motives of the prime movers in the light of subsequent events, we can discover the old design for Mary's overthrow carried out under a new form. Even James Anthony Froude, one of the last men in the world from whom we should expect to hear it, suggests that several at least of the nobles appended their names in deliberate treachery to the Queen.

But where the treachery? I have already pointed out that the attempts to overthrow Mary's authority had hitherto failed chiefly because she was beloved by the people. To succeed against her, therefore, it was necessary to bring her into disgrace before the Scottish nation; and how could this be more successfully done than by drawing her into a marriage with the man who was widely believed to be the murderer of her husband, and then rising up in apparent indignation against the union?

In view of the facts I have just indicated, it is not surprising that, having fallen into the hands of Bothwell, and having been detained by him, Mary should have made the best of the case by consenting to marry him. I do not pretend to decide how far her consent was obtained by persuasion, or how far by force. Both were used. But it should not be forgotten, that for more than six mouths after the event, the public records of Scotland refer to the intercepting of the Queen by Bothwell as a forcible and treasonable act, and speak of her as having been compelled, through fear and other unlawful means, to give her promise of marriage; and it was only when changed circumstances demanded a change of tactics, that the worthies who had hurled her from the throne began to assert that what had been done by Bothwell had been done with her consent. However, leaving aside the question of violence, see what influence persuasion itself could have had. Bothwell was not without certain favourable qualities. His sterling loyalty and great power were invaluable to one in Mary's difficult circumstances. But if these were insufficient to gain his end, there was the agreement signed by the nobles. "And when," writes Mary, giving an account of her marriage to her friends in France, "he saw us like to reject all his suit and offers, in the end he showed us how far he was proceeded with our whole nobility and principals of our estate, and what they had promised him under their handwrits. If we had cause to be astonished, we remit us to the judgment of the King, the Queen, our uncle, and others our friends." Could Mary, with her sore experience of their turbulency, lightly oppose the will of so many of her nobility as set forth in that celebrated "Band?" She might express doubt as to the genuineness of their signatures; but Bothwell could point out that, although she was already in his power nearly twelve days, not one whose name was subscribed thereto had moved hand or foot to liberate her.

If, placed in these circumstances, without any indication that protracted resistance would result in her rescue, she consented to marry Bothwell, is there not sufficient reason for her action, without the theory of an old and ungovernable passion for the "rugged Border Lord"? It is poor philosophy to invent theories to account for events of which we already see adequate cause. Mary may, or may not, have been infatuated with Bothwell; but that she was must be proved--if proved at all--independently of the fact that she married him. In the presumption, warranted by law, reason and common sense, of her innocence, we can account satisfactorily for her marriage. Why then resort to the presumption, warranted neither by law, reason nor common sense, of her guilt, in order to explain it?

It may seem strange that, whatever her circumstances were, she should have married a man who had a wife living. But it must not be forgotten that the Catholic Archbishop of St. Andrews had declared Bothwell's former marriage invalid on the ground of consanguinity within the forbidden degree, from which no dispensation had been obtained. It is true that at a later date Mary regarded her marriage with Bothwell as invalid;[#] but it cannot be inferred that she contracted it in bad faith, for in the meantime doubts may have arisen as to whether the Archbishop's decision was founded on fact.-- A good deal of uncertainty still hangs over the value of this decision. Besides, she must have learned, what does not appear to have occurred to the mind of the Archbishop, that, owing to the ecclesiastical impediment of *raptus*, she was incapable, no matter how earnestly she may have desired it, of contracting valid matrimony with Bothwell, without having first regained his liberty.

[#] I do not think it can be any longer doubted that Mary learned in the course of time to regard her marriage with Bothwell as invalid; and I am surprised that so eminent and enlightened a writer as Mr. Skelton should argue that her "subsequent anxiety to obtain a divorce from Bothwell proves that she continued to believe that the marriage was binding." She was too well versed in Catholic doctrine and in the history of Henry the Eighth's conflict with Rome to hope for a divorce from Bothwell, if she believed the marriage was binding. At any rate, her instructions to Bishop Leslie, whom she sent to Rome in 1575, leave it beyond doubt that it was not a divorce, but merely a declaration that the marriage was null from the beginning, that she asked of the Pope. "Take good heed," she said, "that the Holy Father shall publicly announce that the pretended marriage contracted between me and Bothwell, without any legality but by a pretended procedure is of no (force). For although there are many reasons which, as you know, make it clearly invalid in itself, yet the matter will be much clearer if his Holiness, acting as the most certain lawyer of the Church, will come forward to annul it." (Published from a Cottonian MS. by the late Rev. Joseph Stevenson, S.J., in notes to his preface to Claude Nau's narrative.)

During the nine days that intervened between the times he was brought back to Edinburgh and the day of her marriage, no effort was made to stay the proceedings. Craig, the minister of St. Giles, to whom it fell to publish the marriage banns, courageously declared his disapproval of the union, adding, however, the significant words that "the best part of the realm did approve it, either by flattery or by their silence"--words that show how completely the unfortunate Queen was left under the control of Bothwell.

But as soon as Mary's fortunes were identified with Bothwell's by the bond of marriage, the sound of approaching war was heard. The Confederate lords rose in arms to avenge the murder of the late King (so they said), and to liberate the Queen; and many true friends of Mary's, little suspecting the real purpose of the prime movers, arrayed themselves under their standard. The two armies met at Carberry Hill; no battle ensued. The Confederates promised that if Mary would separate herself from Bothwell and confide in them, they would respect her as their true sovereign. Mary agreed, but once in their power her eyes were opened. She was brought back to Edinburgh, flouted along the way with a banner on which was depicted the effigy of her murdered husband, and exposed to the studied insults of a rabble, half frantic from the fierce harangues of the Knoxonian preachers. The following night she was hurried away, and placed in the lonely castle of Lochleven, situated on a rock in a lake of the same name, in the County of Kinross. And that was how they fulfilled their promises to restore her to her royal estate,--that was her reward for the confidence she had placed in their word.

Froude attempts to justify the action of the Confederates on the ground that Mary, after reaching Edinburgh, refused to give up Bothwell, and that she wrote him a letter which was intercepted that same night, declaring her anxiety to be with him at almost any cost. Of course Froude was not the first to offer this explanation; but no writer who wishes to be classed among respectable historians would now embody that unauthenticated gossip in his narrative in the manner in which Froude has done. Froude evidently relies much on the gullibility of his readers; and not without reason; for how many of those who sweep over his dramatic pages, captivated by the brilliancy of his master style, ever suspect that his statements are reckless and unwarranted?

But did the Confederate lords imprison the Queen because she refused to give up Bothwell? We cannot tell. The alleged letter to Bothwell is the only argument for it, and that letter was never afterwards produced, although the production of it would have been of incalculable value to her enemies. The fact is, the lords gave nobody access to the Queen--not even the English envoy and what she did, or what she desired, we know only through those whose interest it was to make out a case against her.

CHAPTER VII.

CAPTIVITY.--ESCAPE.--FLIGHT.

The next step was to force Mary to abdicate in favour of her infant son. (To use the child against the parent monarch had long been a favourite policy with the Scottish rebel lords.) A delegation was sent to her for that purpose, headed by Lord Lindsay, whom Sir Walter Scott calls "the rudest baron of that rude age"--fit agent for the tyrranous deed. Moved partly by fear that refusal would lead to a violent death, and partly by the previous representation of some of her friends that what she did under constraint could not bind her if she regained her liberty, Mary signed the cruel document--

"She wrote the words--She stood erect--a queen without a crown,"

and although prudence would prevent her from uttering them with her lips, we may be sure that in her heart she spoke the words attributed to her by the poet:--

"My lords,--my lords," the captive said, "were I but once more free,

With ten good knights on yonder shore to aid my cause and me,

That parchment would I scatter wide to every breeze that blows,

And once more reign a Stewart queen o'er my remorseless foes."

The next important visit the helpless Queen received in her prison was from the Earl of Moray. The cautious Earl had been absent in France during the troublous times that had elapsed since the murder of Darnley, but no doubt was well pleased with the success with which Morton and his associates had been advancing his cause. His sister was now dethroned, the infant James was crowned King, and he himself was named Regent. The goal of his ambition seemed near. He had returned to Scotland in time to receive the honours prepared for him, and--whatever his motives were--before formally accepting the Regency, he visited Mary in Lochleven Castle. It is thought by many that he paid this visit with a view to rendering his footing more secure, as he probably hoped that the prisoner, recognizing the helplessness of her condition, would ask him to accept the office of Regent. Depressed with the gravity of the trials she had just passed through, the tender-hearted Queen naturally hoped that her brother's visit would bear some comfort to her lonely prison. But she was disappointed. Ambition (if nothing more) had expelled from Moray's breast those feelings of natural tenderness with which we should presume every man to be moved towards a humiliated and afflicted sister. Even his friends are slow to commend his conduct on this occasion. "That visit" (writes Robertson, in the History of Scotland) "to a sister, and a queen in prison, from which he had neither any intention to relieve her, nor to mitigate the rigour of her confinement, may be mentioned among the circumstances which discover the great want of delicacy and refinement in that age."

As long as the Queen was confined in Lochleven, her friends in Scotland were obliged to keep quiet, for it was intimated to them that if they attempted to liberate her, they would be presented with her head.

The unhappy Queen, cut off from the world in the bloom and beauty of her youth, looked out from day to day across the dull waters that encircled her prison-house, and anxiously surveyed the neighbouring hills in which, she knew, her faithful friends were lingering, in hopes of discovering some means of effecting her deliverance. After various ineffectual attempts, a successful plan of escape was at length devised by the ingenuity of little Willie Douglas, a youth in the household of the Laird of Lochleven.

Sunday, May 2nd, was the day chosen for what proved to be a successful attempt to escape. Lords Seton, Beton and George Douglas, with a number of followers, were lingering about the shore, near the village of Kinross, ready to receive the Queen and convey her to a place of safety. Within the castle prison all preliminaries were arranged, but the lowest point of the wall that Mary could reach was higher than she could venture to leap from, and the keys of the gate were scrupulously guarded by the Laird. Let us hear Nau relate how the problem was solved:--

"An hour before supper-time, the Queen retired into her own chamber. She put on a red kirtle belonging to one of her women, and over it she covered herself with one of her own mantles. Then she went into the garden to talk with the old lady whence she could see the people who were walking on the other side of the loch.

"Everything being now ready, the Queen, who, of set purpose, had caused the supper to be delayed until that time, now ordered it to be served. When the supper was finished, the Laird (whose ordinary custom it was to wait upon her at table), went to sup along with his wife and the rest of the household, in a hall on the ground story. A person called Draisdel,[#] who had the chief charge in the establishment, and who generally remained in the Queen's room to keep her safe, went out along with the Laird, and amused himself by playing at hand ball.

[#] When Draisdel--the original, no doubt, of Scott's imperturbable Dryfesdale in "The Abbott"--was informed by the two young girls that the queen was missing and had probably escaped, "he was amused at this, and said he would soon find her; he would give her leave to escape if she could. At one time he whistled, at another he cut capers." Romance must have been unfair in painting him a phlegmatic steward.

"In order to free herself from the two young girls who remained with her, Her Majesty in the meantime went into an upper room, above her own, occupied by her surgeon, on the plea that she wished to say her prayers; and, indeed, she did pray very devoutly, recommending herself to God, who then showed His pity and care for her. In this room she left her mantle, and, having put on a hood, such as is worn by the country-women of the district, she made one of her domestics, who was to accompany her, dress herself in the same fashion. The other *femme-de-chambre* remained with the two young girls to amuse them, for they had become very inquisitive as to the cause of the Queen's lengthened absence.

"While the laird was at supper, William Douglas, as he was handing him his drink, secretly removed the key of the great gate, which lay on the table before him. He promptly gave notice of this to the Queen, in order that she should come down stairs instantaneously; and immediately afterwards as he came out of the door he gave the sign to the young woman who was to accompany Her Majesty, as she was looking towards the window. This being understood, the Queen came down forthwith; but as she was at the bottom of the steps she noticed that several of the servants of the household were passing backwards and forwards in the court, which induced her to stand for some time the door of the stairs. At last, however, in the sight of the whole of them, she crossed the courtyard, and having gone out by the great gate, William Douglas locked it with the key and threw it into a cannon placed near at hand. The Queen and her *femme-de-chambre* had stood for some time close to the wall, fearing that they should be seen from the windows of the house; but at length they got into the vessel, and the Queen laid herself down under the boatman's seat. She had been advised to do this, partly to escape notice, partly to escape being hit, if a cannon shot should be sent after her. Several washerwomen and other domestics were amusing themselves in a garden near the loch when Her Majesty got into the boat. One of the washerwomen even recognized her, and made a sign to William Douglas that she was aware of it, but William called out to her aloud, by name, telling her to hold her tongue.

"As the boat was nearing the other side, William saw one of George's servants, but failed to recognize him, as he was armed. Apprehending some fraud, he hesitated to come nearer the shore; at length, however, the servant having spoken, he landed, and then Her Majesty was met and welcomed by

George Douglas and John Beton, who had broken into the laird's stables and seized his best horses. Being mounted as best she might, the Queen would not set off until she had seen William Douglas on horse also--he who had hazarded so much for her release. She left her *femme-de-chambre* behind her, but with direction that she should follow her as soon as she could have an outfit."

Being joined by her friends on shore, the Queen hurried south, and, having crossed the Firth at Queen's Ferry, reached Lord Seton's house at Niddry, about midnight. Thence she proceeded to Hamilton, where she remained until the 13th of May collecting her forces. The plan was, to place the Queen in safety in Dunbarton Castle, on the Clyde, and then muster all her forces for the overthrow of the Regent. It is not difficult now to see that her friends made a fatal blunder in not conveying her directly to Dunbarton from Lochleven. In Dunbarton she would be safe, and her followers could take time to properly organize. As it was, those who rallied round her standard during her stay at Hamilton were equal in number to the army under command of the Regent at Glascow. Her two main supports in the North, Lord Ogilvy and the powerful Earl of Huntly, had not yet succeeded in joining her; but the Earls of Argyle, Cassillis, Rothes and Eglinton, Lords Seton, Borthwick, Somerville, Livingstone, Claud Hamilton, Herries, Boyd, Yester, Ross and others, were already at her side. Bravery and chivalry were in her ranks, but organization and efficient generalship were wanting.

The fact that, notwithstanding the persistent and ingenious efforts of her enemies to utterly defame her, so many nobles (most of whom were Protestants), hurried to her support as soon as her escape was made known, draws the following remarks from her Protestant biographer, Mr. Hosack--

"That in spite of all the efforts of Moray and his faction, and in spite of all the violence of the preachers, she--the Catholic Queen of Scotland, the daughter of the hated house of Guise, the reputed mortal enemy of their religion--should now, after being maligned as the most abandoned of her sex, find her best friends among her Protestant subjects, appears at first sight inexplicable. A phenomenon so strange admits of only one explanation. If, throughout her reign, she had not loyally kept her promises of security and toleration to her Protestant subjects, they assuredly would not in her hour of need have risked their lives and fortunes in her defence."

On their march to Dunbarton the Queen's forces were met by those of the Regent at Langside, and thrown into confusion. Attended by three brave nobles--Lords Herries, Fleming and Livingstone--and little Willie Douglas, she hurried towards the south, and, after a wearisome journey, reached Dundrennen Abbey, in Galloway. Here she resolved on a step that was the greatest mistake of her life. The majority of the Scottish people were loyal to her, and only needed time to muster, but in spite of the advice, persuasions and entreaties of Lord Herries and her other attendants, she determined to cross over to England. Elizabeth's recent expressions of friendship and promises of help had blinded the Scottish Queen; and her own generous nature, which would have instantly prompted her to assist, as far as she could, a sister queen in distress, rendered her for the time incapable of suspecting that Elizabeth could betray her in her hour of greatest need. She stepped forth from Scottish soil, never to set foot on it again, and steered across the Firth to the shores of England.

CHAPTER VIII.

IN THE HANDS OF ELIZABETH.

Having landed in England, the Scottish Queen was, by order of Elizabeth, conveyed to Carlisle Castle, and there placed in custody of Sir Francis Knollys. She hastened to send Lord Herries to the English court, to request that Elizabeth, according to her promise, would help restore her to her throne; or at least would give her liberty to pass out of the kingdom and seek help elsewhere. Elizabeth could have pursued either course with honour, but she pursued neither; and as long as right is right and wrong is wrong--as long as justice is not synonymous with temporal advantage--so long will it remain impossible to frame a defence for Elizabeth Tudor in her conduct toward Mary Stewart. Her hostility to Mary, and her support of Mary's enemies, veil them as she would, were evident throughout the subsequent proceedings.

Mary's friends in Scotland were rising in large numbers and preparing to take the field against the Regent. Elizabeth, leading Mary to believe that she would reinstate her, prevailed on her to request her partizans to desist from warfare; the Regent in the meantime continued his work of destruction against those who had fought for the Queen. Elizabeth offered to act as umpire between the Regent's party and Mary. The whole affair, so Mary was given to understand, would turn out to her profit. Thomas Howard, Duke of Norfolk; Thomas Ratcliff, Earl of Sussex, and Sir Ralph Sadler, were nominated commissioners by Elizabeth to hear the charge of political misgovernment which the Regent would bring against Mary. No charge affecting Mary's personal honour was to be admitted.

The conference opened at York, in October, 1568. Of course it was mere fiction to speak of Mary's misgovernment. But would Cecil and Elizabeth lose their opportunity of disgracing, as far as they could, the Scottish Queen, in the eyes of the English people, and of rendering a compromise with her enemies in Scotland impossible? Such could hardly be expected. The Conference was transferred to Westminster, and, contrary to the conditions on which Mary had permitted her case to be referred to a commission, Moray was assured that he might bring forward accusations against her honour--in fact he was urged or encouraged to do so. He then accused her of being the author, with Bothwell, of her late husband's murder, and of having intended a like fate for her infant son; and in support of his charge he produced the celebrated documents known as the Casket Letters, consisting of letters and sonnets which, he claimed, had been written by Mary to Bothwell, and had fallen into the hands of the Earl of Morton, shortly after the surrender at Carberry Hill. Mary's commissioners protested against this violation of the conditions on which the conference had been opened, and demanded that, as Moray had been admitted to Elizabeth's presence, so should their Queen. Otherwise, they maintained, the conference was closed. Cecil disregarded their protests, and the Regent placed his accusations and papers before the commissioners and Lords of the Privy Council. Mary, hearing this, instructed her commissioners to declare that Moray himself and his faction were guilty of Darnley's murder, and that if she were furnished with the originals or even with copies of the Casket Letters, and admitted to the presence of Elizabeth as her accusers had been, she should prove them to be liars, and should convict certain persons of their number as the real murderers. But she was refused admittance to Queen Elizabeth. As soon as she was informed of the refusal, she directed her commissioners to resume the conference, and to throw back the charge of murder on Moray and his associates. But the conference was not resumed, nor was Mary furnished with the originals of the letters that had been brought forward as evidence against her honour. Elizabeth, Cecil and Moray shrank from a fair investigation of the case; and Moray, with his "Casket" and "Originals," and with £5,000 of Elizabeth's gold in his pocket, was hurried back to Scotland. Mary, however, was left as before--a prisoner whom Elizabeth would neither help to regain her throne, nor permit to pass out of the realm. Matters now seemed to stand in the condition in which Elizabeth had hoped to place them. The breach between Mary and the Regent's party had been rendered irreparable; and the English nation--in which she had had so many adherents--had been taught (so at least her enemies hoped), to regard the Scottish Queen as a criminal and abandoned woman.

The celebrated Casket Letters demand at least a brief consideration. If they are genuine, Mary was undoubtedly implicated in the murder of her husband. If they are forged or interpolated, they are not only worthless as evidence against her, but are a crowning proof of her innocence. Much of the matter of these letters might have been written by Mary--and probably was written by her, though not to Bothwell--without being evidence that she shared in the murder. It is commonly believed by her friends that the Casket Letters are partly made up of letters written by her to Darnley. It is well known that, while she was in Lochleven, Holyrood was ransacked by the Morton-Moray faction, and that her papers, as well as those which Darnley may have left there, were at their disposal. They could easily select those letters which could be most readily doctored up so as to bear a sinister meaning, and those which, as they stood, would appear criminal if addressed to other than Darnley. There is, however, one letter, or at least part of one letter, that could not be written by Mary if she was innocent, namely, letter No. 2, represented as written to Bothwell from Glasgow, while she was visiting Darnley in his sickness.

With regard to these letters, I would say, in the first place, that they cannot be adduced as conclusive evidence of Mary's guilt, because, at best, their genuineness is doubtful. I would say, in the second place, that at any rate as far as the incriminating portions are concerned, I cannot regard them as other than forged; and here in brief are my principal reasons for rejecting them:--

First. Because, in view of the ill-treatment to which in other things she was subjected, and of the unfair tactics used against her, by those interested in producing the Casket Letters, no accusation proceeding from that same source against her honour as a woman, can be accepted, unless it is clearly substantiated. It can hardly be controverted that, whatever Mary's faults may have been, the Morton-Moray faction had already treated her dishonourably and unjustly. They had plotted with foreigners against her before ever the Bothwell imbroglio arose; they had tried to brand her with dishonour at the time of the Rizzio murder; they had broken their promise, given at Carberry Hill, and had cast her into prison; they had brutally forced her to abdicate, and then, in open Parliament, solemnly professed that she had voluntarily resigned. Besides, the Earl of Morton, whose testimony is the principal evidence in support of the genuineness of the Casket Letters, was probably the most vicious and unscrupulous man in Scotland. Can the testimony of such men,--men who had acknowleged that they had gone too far to recede,--given to protect their most cherished interests, to defend perhaps their very lives, be accepted as conclusive evidence, where there are so many evident reasons to suspect their veracity?

Second. Because these letters, and these letters only, exhibit in Mary an indelicacy of language, and a jestful levity in treating of crime, which are altogether foreign to her character as learned from reliable and authentic sources.

Third. Because a score, or thereabouts, of the most distinguished Scottish peers, in the instructions which they issued in September, 1568, to Mary's commissioners in England, declared that at least the incriminating portions of these letters were not in the Queen's handwriting. This valuable document recounts clearly and briefly the history of the disturbance which had ended in Mary's overthrow, and exposes, according to the view of the subscribers, the deceitful conduct of her enemies. I am not aware of any external evidence bearing on the Casket Letters that can compare in force and authority with this document. Whoever is acquainted with the history of the Scottish nobility of that time, must admit that the men whose names are subscribed thereto were at least as honest and honourable as the leaders of the Regent's party; and that the vindication of the Queen's honour would be no more profitable to them than her complete overthrow would be to those who had usurped her power and authority. Now these instructions state, in express terms, what many other evidences, both internal and external, have since gone to establish, that, however much of the Casket literature was Mary's the compromising parts had been interpolated by her enemies. "If it be alleged" (thus the instructions) "that Her Majesty's writing produced in Parliament should prove culpable, it may be answered that there is no place mention made in it by which she may be convicted, albeit it were her own hand-writing--*which it is not*--and also the same is devised by themselves in some principal and substantial clauses."

Fourth. Because the papers that were passed off as the originals in Mary's hand-writing were kept out of sight and, far as can be known, were seen, neither then nor since, by anybody except the select few at Hampton Court; and though Mary repeatedly demanded them, they were never shown her.

Fifth. Another document, represented as a warrant from the Queen requiring the lords to sign the celebrated Anslie tavern "band" for her marriage with Bothwell, was said to be in the Casket also, and was furtively shown in the Conference at York, but was never produced in the official enquiry at Westminster. The suppression of such a document, which, by reason of its public nature, could easily have been proved genuine, if it really were so, seems to admit of only one explanation--it could not stand the light of criticism, it was forged. But if the other Casket papers were genuine, Mary's accusers had no need of forged ones.

Sixth. The Casket Letter number two, commonly known as the Glascow letter (because it was supposed to have been written to Bothwell from Glasgow while Mary was visiting her sick husband there) contains a report of a conversation between Mary and Darnley which corresponds so closely with another document adduced eighteen months later in evidence against the Queen, that the one must have been copied from the other. A brief explanation is necessary to make the importance of this circumstance clear. A certain Robert Crawfurd was in attendance on Darnley at Glasgow when Mary went thither to comfort him. At the request of the Earl of Lennox, Darnley's father, Crawfurd (so he states), noted down the conversations that passed between the royal couple; but, not being present at them, he learned what had been said only from the account which Darnley afterwards gave him. Also in the letter number two is recounted one of Darnley's plaintive discourses. It is clear, therefore, that if it could be shown that the conversation embodied in this letter was really held, something would be done to give an air of genuineness to the whole document. Hence, Crawfurd was called upon for an account of what had passed between Mary and Darnley, and his deposition was brought forward by the Regent and his associates before the English commissioners. Now, it turns out that Crawfurd's deposition and the portion of the Casket Letter that covers the same ground, agree almost verbally--agree, in fact, so wonderfully that, all the circumstances considered, it is impossible to resist the conclusion that either one must have been copied from the other, and that a fraud was practised somewhere, for both documents were represented as original. I have said, "all the circumstances considered." We must remember that reporters, especially if they are not skilled stenographers, recording a speech, even, while it is being delivered, exhibit a considerable divergence of vocabulary and phraseology in their respective reports. But here both Crawfurd and Mary reported from memory; in fact, Crawfurd had to struggle against the vagaries of two memories--his own and Darnley's. This is what makes the agreement suspiciously strange. More than that; Crawfurd's deposition was written in Scots, while the Casket letter was written in French, and afterwards translated into Scots; and it is these two documents which, in spite of so many causes why they should widely differ, are found to agree so closely.

Here are the passages in question:--

Deposition of Crawfurd.

"Ye asked me what I ment by the crueltye specified in my lettres; yat proceedethe of you onelye, that wille not accept mye offres and repentance. I confess that I have failed in som thingis, and yet greater faultes have bin made to you sundrye tymes, which ye have forgiven. I am but yonge, and ye will saye ye have forgiven me diverse tymes. Maye not a man of mye age, for lack of counselle, of which I am very destitute, falle twise or thrise, and yet repent, and be chastised bye experience? If I have made any faile that ye wul think a faile, howsoever its be, I crave your pardone, and protest that I shall never faile againe. I desire no other thinge but that we may be together as husband and wife. And if ye will not consent hereto, I desire never to ris futhe from this bed. Therefore I pray yow, give me an answer hereunto. God knoweth how I am punished for making mye god of yow, and for having no other thought but on yow. And if at ainie tyme I offend yow, ye are the cause; for that when anie offendethe me, if for mye refuge I might open mye minde to you, I would speak to no other; but when ainie thing is spoken to me, and ye and I not beinge as husband and wife ought to be, necessitee compelleth me to kepe it in my brest," etc.

Alleged Letter of Mary's.

(Translated from French into Scots.)

"Ye ask me quhat I mene be the crueltie conteint in my letter; it is of you alone, that will not accept my offeris and repentance. I confess that I have faillit but not into that quihilk I ever denyit; and sicklyke hes faillit to sindrie of your subjeetis, quhilk ye have forgiven. I am young. Ye will say that ye have forgiven me ofttymes, and yit yat I return to my faultis. May not ane man of my age, for lack of counsell, fall twyse or thryse, or in lack of his promeis, and at last repent himself, and be chastisit be experience? If I may obtain pardoun, I proteste I shall never make faulte agane. And I craif na uther thing bot yat we may be at bed and buird togidder as husband and wyfe; and gif ye will not consent heirunto I sail nevir ryse out of yis bed. I pray yow tell me yoor resolution. God knawis how I am punischit for making my god of yow, and for having na uther thoucht bot on yow; and gif at ony tyme I offend yow, ye are the caus; because when ony offendis me, gif for my refuge I micht playne unto yow, I would speike it unto na uther body; but quhen I heir ony thing, not being familiar with you, necessitie constraine me to keip it in my briest," etc.

It will be noticed that, not only are the words the same (the differences of spelling do not affect the case), but the clauses and phrases occupy the same relative positions in both documents. And yet we are asked to believe that these are independent reports of the same discourse, written down from memory.

A distinguished Scottish writer has summed up the question thus: "That Mary and Darnley should have held a long private conversation on many topics of no particular importance; that after Mary was gone Darnley should have repeated the whole conversation to Crawfurd; that Crawfurd either then or eighteen months later should have written out a report in Scots of what Darnley had said; that Mary should have written within twenty-four hours a letter in French in which she also reported the conversation; that Mary's letter should have been afterwards translated into Scots; and that the Scots translation of Mary's letter should have been found to agree, word for word, with Crawfurd's report,--this series of marvels is more than the most devout credulity can stomach." (John Skelton, C.B., LL.D.)

Seventh. The history of these letters makes it tolerably clear that it was many months after they were said to have been discovered by Morton, before they took definite form; in other words, that they were being concocted, at least, to use the words of the loyal nobility, "in some principal and substantial clauses." Even as late as the month of August, 1567, the rebel lords reiterated that Bothwell had laid violent hands on the Queen, and that they had risen up to rescue her from his thraldom. But on December 4th, the same lords declared, as we read in the Act of the Secret Counsel, that they had taken arms against her because she was an accomplice of Bothwell's in the murder of her husband, as shown "be divers hir previe lettres written and subscrivit with hir awen hand, and sent by hir to James Erll Boithwell." This flat contradiction between the statements of the same parties arouses the strongest suspicion of treachery. Nor will it avail to say that in their excessive charity, they had for a time chosen to make liars of themselves rather than unnecessarily reveal the vices of their former Queen; for, according to the deposition of Morton, at least according to what Mary's adversaries claim to be Morton's deposition, the Casket containing the incriminating documents was taken from a servant of Bothwell's on June 20th--nearly two weeks after the Confederate lords had taken up arms. Again, the minutes of the Secret Counsel describe the letters as "written and subscrit with hir (Mary's) awen hand, and sent by hir to James Erll Boithwell." Yet the letters exhibited at Hampton Court nearly a year later, were neither signed by Mary, nor addressed to Bothwell.

Eighth. The Countess of Lennox, Darnley's mother, has indirectly furnished evidence against the genuineness of the Casket Letters that can scarcely be valued too highly. For some years she had ceased to be on friendly terms with the Queen. It was her husband, the Earl, who had demanded that Bothwell should be tried for the murder of their son; and by reason of the suspicions which fanatical clamour and cunning treachery had attached to Mary's conduct, the bereaved parents had naturally entertained bitter feelings for their royal daughter-in-law. But the villainy which had brought the unfortunate Queen to an English prison was at length revealed; close acquaintance with the Regent Morton, the quondam leading spirit of the rebel faction, afforded the Countess opportunities of discovering facts that neither she nor her husband had known during the strife of 1567; and, in November, 1575, she comforted the imprisoned exile by a letter in which, among other things, she said:--

"I beseech Your Majesty, fear not, but trust in God that all shall be well; the treachery of your traitors is known better than before. I shall always play my part to Your Majesty's content, willing God, so as may ten to both our comforts." "*The treachery of your traitors is known better than before.*" Could the mother of the murdered King change front and write thus, if she believed that Mary had written the Casket Letter number two, in all its parts?

CHAPTER IX.

THE QUEEN OF SCOTS DETAINED A PRISONER.

Mary's cause, as far as Elizabeth was concerned, was now hopeless, although the unfortunate Queen was not given to understand as much. She was removed from Carlisle, which was too near her English friends and her faithful Scottish Borderers. The danger of leaving her at Carlisle is thus hinted by Mr. Skelton, where he describes the effect she produced on Sir Francis Knollys:--

"When she first flashed upon him in her dishevelled beauty and strong anger--travel-stained though she was from her long ride after the Langside panic--the puritanic veteran warmed into unpremeditated welcome. When we read the remarkable letters in which he describes the fugitive Queen, we cease to wonder at the disquietude of Elizabeth; a glance, a smile, a few cordial words, from such a woman might have set all the northern counties in a blaze. The cold and canny Scot, whose metaphysical and theological ardour contrast so curiously with his frugal common sense, could stolidly resist the charm; but the Catholic nobles, the Border chivalry, would have responded without a day's delay to her summons."

It will not be amiss to give, as recorded from time to time in his own words, the impression which the fugitive and impassioned Queen made on Sir Francis during the short time she was under his care.

"We found her," he writes, "in her chamber of presence ready to receive us, when we declared unto her Your Highness' (Queen Elizabeth's) sorrowfulness for her lamentable misadventure. We found her in answer to have an eloquent tongue and a discreet head; and it seemeth by her doings she hath stout courage and liberal heart adjoining thereto." Later: "This lady and princess is a notable woman. She seemeth to regard no ceremonious honour besides the acknowledgment of her estate royal. She showeth a disposition to speak much, to be bold, to be pleasant, to be very familiar. She showeth a great desire to be revenged of her enemies. She shows a readiness to expose herself to all perils in hope of victory. She desires much to hear of hardiness and valiancy, commending by name all approved hardy men of her country, although they be her enemies; and she concealeth no cowardice even in her friends. The thing she most thirsteth after is victory; and it seemeth to be indifferent to her to have her enemies diminished either by the sword of her friends, or by the liberal promises and rewards of her purse, or by division and quarrels among themselves. So that for victory's sake, pain and peril seem pleasant to her; and in respect of victory, wealth and all things seem to her contemptuous and vile. Now what is to be done with such a lady and princess, and whether such a lady and princess is to be nourished in our bosom, or whether it be good to halt and dissemble with such a lady, I refer to your judgment. The plainest way is the most honorable in my opinion." Yes; "the plainest way is the most honourable," but "to halt and dissemble" was esteemed the most profitable. Again Knollys writes: "She does not dislike my plain dealing. Surely she is a rare woman; for as no flattery can lightly abuse her, so no plain speech seemeth to offend her, if she think the speaker thereof to be an honest man." If we knew nothing of Mary but what we have learned from the pen of this cold and critical adversary, who saw her only when misfortune and disappointment might well have soured and irritated her nature, yet found her "eloquent, discreet, bold, pleasant, very familiar," unmoved by flattery and unruffled by "plain speech," we could legitimately infer that fascinating beyond all ordinary measure must have been the days of her unclouded girlhood in France, and even the less cheerful years of her prosperity in Holyrood;[#] and we could well understand why Elizabeth--who hated her for her claim to the English throne and for her surpassing personal beauty--was anxious to place her as far as possible beyond reach of her friends and sympathizers. The necessity of doing this was emphasized nearly a year later, when Mary was at Tutbury in charge of the Earl of Shrewsbury, by a certain friend of Cecil's named Nicholas White, whose curiosity had lead him to seek an audience with the far-famed captive. In a letter to Cecil, which, as its parenthetical clauses clearly demonstrate, was intended also for the eye of Elizabeth, he wrote:--

[#] Randolph, the English Ambassador to Scotland, has left us, in a letter to Queen Elizabeth, a lively picture of the Scottish queen at the age of twenty-two. He had waited on her at St. Andrews, whither she had withdrawn to pass a few quiet days with some friends, and he describes how good-humouredly she upbraided him for interrupting their merriment with his "grave matters." Among other things he wrote:--"Immediately after the receipt of your letter to this Queen, I repaired to St. Andrews. So soon as time served, I did present the same, which being read, and as appeared in her countenance very well liked, she said little to me for that time. The next day she passed wholly in mirth, nor gave any appearance to any of the contrary; nor would not, as she said openly, but be quiet and merry. Her grace lodged in a merchant's house, her train were very few; and there was small repair from any part. Her will was, that for the time that I did tarry, I should dine and sup with her. Your Majesty was aftertimes dranken unto by her, at dinners and suppers. Having in this sort continued with her grace Sunday, Monday, and Tuesday, I thought it time to take occasion to utter unto her grace that which last I received in command from your Majesty, by Mr. Secretary's letter.... I had no sooner spoken these words, but she saith, I see now well that you are weary of this company and treatment. I sent for you to be merry, and to see how like a Bourgeois wife I live with my little troop; and you will interrupt our pastime with your great and grave matters. I pray you, sir, if you weary here, return home to Edinburgh, and keep your gravity and great embassade until the Queen come thither; for I assure you, you shall not get her here, nor I know not myself where she is gone; you see neither cloth nor estate, nor such appearance that you may think that there is a queen here; nor I would not that you should think that I am she, at St. Andrews, that I was at Edinburgh."

"If I (who in the sight God bear the Queen's majesty a natural love beside my bounded duty) might give advice, there should be very few subjects in this land have access to, or conference with, this lady. For besides that she is a goodly personage (and yet in truth not comparable to our Sovereign), she hath withal an alluring grace, a pretty Scottish speech, and a searching wit, clouded with mildness." We are indebted to Mr. White for the following piece of information also: "Her hair of itself is black; and yet Mr. Knollys told me that she wears hair of sundry colours."

From this time forward Mary's history is the history of sustaining hope and depressing disappointment. Hopes of an accommodation with her rebel subjects were held out to her by Elizabeth; non-committal promises of her restoration were made; kill-time negotiations were sometimes entered into. It is distressing to read the history of her nineteen years of imprisonment. She never ceased to hope for her release, and yet her hopes were repeatedly disappointed. She continued to write Elizabeth in a friendly tone, hoping, no doubt, to touch a chord of sympathy in her cousin's heart; but she never cringed, she never abased herself. The proud spirit of her forefathers, which she had so fully inherited, lent courage and dignity to her utterances. Various plans were laid for her rescue; but her great distance from any point from which she could be carried out of the realm, rendered them ineffectual. She was removed from place to place, more than a dozen times. The close confinement and the advance of years began to tell on her once lithe and beautiful form. And, indeed, what suffering could be more terrible to a young woman of Mary's lively temperament, than prolonged confinement under a rigorous regime and complete separation from the society of friends. No wonder the Bard of Ayr indignantly addresses Elizabeth:--

The weeping blood in woman's breast

Was never known to thee,

Nor the balm that draps on wound of woe

Frae woman's pitying e'e.

If Mary continued to languish in an English prison, it was not because the majority of the Scottish people had not the good-will to liberate her and place her on the throne. But now, as in the days of her imprisonment in Lochleven Castle, the very love they bore her paralyzed their efforts in her behalf. A miscarried attempt at rescuing her would most probably involve the loss of her life. Elizabeth had received assurance that Mary would never be allowed to pass the precincts of her prison alive. The most distinguished and powerful nobles in Scotland--Argyll, Huntly, Chatelheraut, Athol, Herries, and many others--continued to support her cause, and there is hardly room to doubt, that if Scotland had been left to settle its own internal disputes, Mary would have been restored. But Elizabeth was resolved that Scotland should not settle its own disputes. She laid aside the mask, when she could no longer wear it, and, according as the need arose, sent her soldiers into Scotland to help overpower the friends of Mary. From the day on which Moray returned to Scotland from the Westminster farce, the Queen's party began to gain strength. But what could this avail, since Elizabeth was determined that the cause of the helpless captive should not prosper. The Regent was shot at Linlithgow in January, 1570, and the Earl of Lennox, who succeeded him in the Regency, gave notice to the Ambassador of Elizabeth that English aid would be necessary for the maintenance of his position. The aid, of course, was granted, and the English auxiliaries, under Sussex, by the severity which they exercised against the adherents of the Queen, fully demonstrated their claim to the title of "auld enemies." Mary's party had done enough to prove their loyalty, but when Elizabeth unreservedly cast her lot with the opposite side, they could not hope for permanent success, and they ultimately came to terms with the Regent.

The disgust which Moray's conduct towards his sister had excited among the moderate Scottish nobles is apparent in the action of two leading personages, shortly after the breaking up of the Westminster Conference. William Maitland of Lethington--the "flower of Scottish wit"--and William Kirkaldy of Grange--the "mirror of chivalry"--had been attached to the Regent's party, although it is certain that at least Maitland aimed at a compromise with the Queen and opposed extreme measures. Seeing that a middle course was no longer possible, they unequivocally went over to the Queen's party. Kirkaldy was Governor of Edinburgh Castle, and in April, 1571, Maitland, broken down in body, but mentally the recognized leader of the Queen's men, passed within its walls. From this inacessible height Kirkaldy could look down with indifference on the futile efforts of the Regent's forces to dislodge him, and Maitland could send forth to his associates his letters of advice and encouragement. Throughout the country the opposing forces met in many a bloody conflict. Lennox was killed in an engagement with Huntly in 1571; the Earl of Mar, who succeeded him, died the following year, and the Regency passed into the hands of the fierce and licentious Earl of Morton.

Morton renewed the conflict with redoubled vigour. But Kirkaldy's position remained impregnable. "Mons. Meg," the old monster gun, so famous in Scottish history, continued to roar defiance from the ramparts of the Castle, and the Standard of Mary still floated over David's tower. But the old story was repeated; English troops were sent from Berwick to reinforce Morton; and on May the 9th, 1573, the Castle surrendered.

In England the sympathy for the fallen Queen had already burst forth in sudden but ill-directed revolt, under the leadership of two of the most ancient and powerful peers of the realm,--the Earls of Northumberland and Westmorland. Slight success at the outset was soon succeeded by disorder and disaster. The Earls fled to Scotland, whence Westmorland passed safely to Flanders. Northumberland was taken by the Regent Moray, and was afterwards, to the great disgust and humiliation of all honest Scotsmen, handed over to Elizabeth by the Regent Morton, in return for a suitable sum of money. Needless to say the Earl was put to death. Sir Walter Scott, always ready to view transaction from the standpoint of chivalry, makes the following reference to this bargain:--

"The surrender of this unfortunate nobleman to England was a great stain, not only on the character of Morton, but on that of Scotland in general, which had hitherto been accounted a safe and hospitable place of refuge for those whom misfortune or political faction had exiled from their own country. It was the more particularly noticed because when Morton himself had been forced to fly to England, on account of his share in Rizzio's murder, he had been courteously received and protected by the unhappy nobleman whom he had now delivered up to his fate. It was an additional and aggravating circumstance, that it was a Douglas who had betrayed a Percy,[#] and when the annals of their ancestors were considered, it was found that while they presented many acts of open hostility, many instances of close and firm alliance, they never till now had afforded an example of any act of treachery exercised by one family against the other. To complete the infamy of the transaction, a sum of money was paid to the Regent on this occasion, which he divided with Douglas of Lochleven." (*Tales of a Grandfather.*)

[#] Northumberland was a Percy; Westmoreland, a Nevil.

On February 4th, 1568, Mary passed to the care of the Earl of Shrewsbury, who was destined to be her keeper for the next fifteen years. In November, 1570, she was brought to Sheffield where she was detained, almost without interruption, for fourteen years. Personally, Shrewsbury bore no ill-will to his charge. He appears to have been an upright and cultured man, and was evidently disposed to treat his prisoner with the consideration and leniency her rank and misfortune would seem to demand. But he was a loyal subject of Elizabeth's, and until she should be pleased to relieve him of his unpleasant duty, he would faithfully execute her will in regard to the restrictions which she thought fit to place on the liberty of the Scottish Queen.

Great as were the bodily and mental sufferings which close confinement, disappointed hopes and the ingratitude of men produced, they would have been greatly aggravated, had Mary only known by what a slender thread her life sometimes hung. Elizabeth entered into negotiations with successive Regents, from Moray to Morton, for the delivery of Mary into their hands. The remonstrances of the French and Spanish Ambassadors, who represented that such an action would be equivalent to condemning her to instant death, arrested the progress of the first negotiations till the death of Moray brought them to an abrupt ending. During the regency of Mar, the project was revived and almost realized, the necessary condition that Mary should be quickly put to death having been agreed to by the Regent and Morton. But here the death of another Regent intervened to save the doomed Queen from assassination or judicial murder. On the death of Mar, Morton, who had hitherto been the real, though not the nominal Regent, assumed the reins of government. He had no scruples about executing the will of Elizabeth, but he demanded a higher price for his services than she cared to pay. Morton and Elizabeth were well matched; they both knew the value of money, and were unwilling to close a bargain that would not promise to be a safe business transaction. Morton was, no doubt, confident that he would not be hampered by competition in the work he was undertaking, and that he could exact what wages he pleased for his expert labour. Killegrew, the agent of Elizabeth, understood this, and was anxious that the bargain should be clinched before Morton took it into his mind to demand a greater reward. "I pray God," he wrote; "we prove not herein like those who refused the three volumes of Sibylla's prophecies, with the price that they were afterwards pleased to give for one; for sure I left the market here better cheap than now I find it." But Elizabeth would not be outwitted--and Mary lived on.

A never-failing source of sorrow to Mary was the knowledge that her son, whom she had seen for the last time an infant, scarcely twelve months old, at Stirling, was in charge of those who had contrived her own overthrow, and was under the tutorship of the venal and ungrateful Buchanan. The burden of her captivity would have been immeasurably lightened, could she have been assured that he had learned to love her and feel for her misfortunes. But the young James, whatever may have been his desire, was in the hands of her enemies, and could communicate with his mother only in the manner and through the means that they were pleased to specify. Nevertheless, as he grew older he had ample opportunity of learning the real character of the men who had dethroned her, and would, it must be presumed, have done what he could to procure her release, did not the promptings of human interest run counter to the dictates of natural love. He was not of that stuff of which heroes are made. The bravery and chivalry for which his forefathers had long been distinguished, found no abode in his bosom. A sound skin and the prospect of succeeding to the English throne weighed more with him than the thought of adopting a firm and uncompromising policy in defence of his mother. While the projects of Mary's friends on the Continent gave promise of being carried to a successful issue, he was not averse to plotting with the Guises and seeking the aid of the Pope in behalf of his "dearest and most honoured lady mother"; but when these projects came to naught, he was found closely allied to the winning cause. Later on, it is true, when Mary was declared a party to a conspiracy against the life of Elizabeth, and her execution was imminent, he dispatched Ambassadors to the English Court to intercede for her life; and when at last the fatal blow was struck, he gave vent to angry feelings and expressed a desire of revenge. A large number of the Scottish nobility were anxious to avert by armed force the contemplated insult to their nation, and to secure Scotland against a humiliation such as their ancestors would never have tolerated. But a cowardly King and a divided nobility were not the forces which, in earlier days, had awakened terror in the heart of England. Elizabeth and her advisers know this, and were well aware that the fear of never reaching the goal of his ambition--the united thrones of England and Scotland--would curb within harmless limits the half-hearted anger of the selfish James.

CHAPTER X.

ELIZABETH UNMOVED BY HER CAPTIVE'S APPEALS.

Reading the history of Mary's prison life in England, one is surprised at the frequent expressions of hope in Elizabeth's good will which are found in her letters. How she could continue to hope in one who had repeatedly deceived her is difficult to explain, except on the supposition that she was constitutionally incapable of believing that misery such as hers could fail to awaken sympathy in the heart of a woman. There can be little doubt, however, that she believed considerably less in Elizabeth's friendship than she professed. But the absence of all well-founded hope, except through the favourable action of Elizabeth, led her to employ every subtle means in her power to induce her "good cousin" to break the fetters of her captivity, and restore her once more to liberty. Still, she did not always restrain her actions within these diplomatic lines; she was human,--noble and courageous, it is true, but only human--and the desire of freedom, the sense of the injustice she suffered, and the pains of her illness, occasionally broke forth in angry and impassioned language. But she never lost the consciousness that she was a Queen, nor did she hesitate, when mild and guarded language proved vain, to speak with bold and dignified straightforwardness, that seemed almost designed to challenge the direst resentment of her royal captor. Her letter to Elizabeth, dated from Sheffield, November 8th, 1582, is a good specimen, both of her plain, outspoken style, and of her insinuating pathos, and likewise witnesses the clearness and vigour of her mind, despite long years of bodily and mental suffering. The document is lengthy, and I shall omit those paragraphs which I may consider of lesser interest to the reader:--

"Madam,--

"Upon that which has come to my knowledge of the last conspiracies executed in Scotland against my poor child, having reason to fear the consequence of it, from the example of myself; I must employ the very small remainder of my life and strength before my death, to discharge my heart to you fully of my just and melancholy complaints, of which I desire that this letter may serve you, as long as you live after me, for a perpetual testimony and engraving upon your conscience; as much for my discharge to posterity as to the shame and confusion of all those who, under your approbation, have so cruelly and unworthily treated me to this time, and reduced me to the extremity in which I am. But, as their designs, practices, actions and proceedings, though as detestable as they could have been, have always prevailed with you against my very just remonstrances, and sincere deportment; and as the power which you have in your hands, has always been a reason for you among mankind, I will have recourse to the living God, our only judge, who has established us equally and immediately under him for the government of his people.

"I will invoke to the end of this, my very pressing affliction, that he will return to you, and to me (as he will do in his last judgment), the share of our merits, and demerits, one towards the other. And remember, Madam, that to him we shall not be able to disguise anything by the paint and policy of the world; though mine enemies, under you, have been able, for a time, to cover their subtle inventions to men, perhaps to you.

"In his name, and before him sitting, between you and me, I will remind you, that by the agents, spies and secret messengers sent in your name into Scotland while I was there, my subjects were corrupted and encouraged to rebel against me, *to make attempts upon my person*, and, in one word to speak, to emprise and execute that which has come to the said country during my troubles. Of which I will not at present specify other proof than that which I have gained of it by the confession of one who was afterwards amongst those that were most advanced for this good service, and of the witnesses confronted with him. To whom, if I had since done justice, he had not afterwards, by his ancient intelligences, renewed the same practices against my son, and had not procured for all my traitorous and rebellious subjects, who took refuge with you, that aid and support which they have had ever since my detention on this side (i. e., in England); without which support, I think, the said traitors could not since have prevailed, nor afterwards have stood out so long as they have done.

"During my imprisonment at Lochleven, Trogmorton counselled me on your behalf to sign that demission, which he advertised me would be presented to me, assuring me that it could not be valid. And there was not afterwards a place in Christendom where it was held for valid, except on this side, where it was maintained, even to have assisted with open force, the authors of it. In your conscience, Madam, would you acknowledge an equal liberty and power in your subjects? Notwithstanding this, my authority has been by my subjects transferred to my son, when he was not capable of exercising it.

"When I was escaped from Lochleven, ready to give battle to my rebels, I remitted to you, by a gentleman, express a diamond jewel, which I had formerly received as a token from you, and with assurance to be succoured by you against my rebels; and even that, on my retiring towards you, you would come to the very frontiers in order to assist me, which had been confirmed to me by divers messengers. This promise coming, and repeatedly, from your mouth (though I had found myself often abused by your Ministers), made me place such affiance on the effectiveness of it that, when my army was routed, I came directly to throw myself into your arms, if I had been able to approach them. But while I was planning to set out to find you, there was I arrested on my way, surrounded with guards, secured in strong places, and at last reduced, all shame set aside, to the captivity in which I remain to this day, after a thousand deaths which I have already suffered for it.

* * * * *

"In the meantime my rebels, perceiving that their headlong course was carrying them much farther than they had thought before, and the truth being evidenced concerning the calumnies that had been propagated of me at the conference, to which I submitted, in full assembly of your deputies and mine, with others of the contrary party in that country, in order to clear myself publicly of them; there were the principals,[#] for having come to repentance, besieged by your forces in the Castle of Edinburgh, and one of the first among them poisoned, and the other most cruelly hanged, after I had twice made them lay down their arms, at your request, in hopes of an agreement which God knows whether my enemies aimed at, I have been for a long time trying whether patience would soften the rigour and ill-treatment, which they have begun, for these ten years particularly, to make me suffer. And accommodating myself exactly to the order prescribed me for my captivity in this house, as well in regard to the number and quality of the attendants, which I retain, dismissing the others; as for my diet, and ordinary exercise for my health, I am living, even at present, as quietly and peaceably as one much inferior to myself, and more obliged, than with such treatment, I was to you, had been able to do; even to deprive myself, in order to take away all shadow of suspicion and diffidence from you, of requiring to have some intelligence with my son, and my country, which is what, by no right or reason, could be denied me, and principally with my child; whom, instead of this, they have endeavoured by every way to persuade against me, in order to weaken us by our division.

[#] Secretary Maitland and the Laird of Grange, whose defection from the Regent's party has already been mentioned.

"It was permitted me, you will say, to send one to visit him there, about three years ago. His captivity then at Stirling, under the tyrany of Morton, was the cause of it; as his liberty was afterwards, of a refusal to make the like visit. All this year past I have several times entered into divers overtures for the establishment of a good amity between us, and a sure understanding between these realms in future. To Chatsworth, about ten years ago, commissioners were sent for that purpose. A treaty had been held upon it with yourself, by my ambassadours and those of France. I even myself made, concerning it, the last winter, all the advantageous overtures to Beal that it was possible to make. What return have I had thence? My good intention has been despised, the sincerity of my actions has been neglected and calumniated, the state of my affairs has been traversed by delays, postponings and other such artifices. And, in conclusion, a worse and more unworthy treatment from day to day, anything which I am compelled to do in order to deserve the contrary, my very long, useless and prejudicial patience, have rendered me so low that mine enemies, in their habits of using me ill, think this day they have the right of prescription for treating me, not as a prisoner, which, in reason I could not be, but as some slave whose life and whose death depend only upon their tyrrany.

"I cannot, Madam, suffer it any longer; and I must in dying, discover the authors of my death, or, living, attempt, under your protection, to find an end to the cruelties, calumnies and traitorous designs of my said enemies, in order to establish me in some little more repose for the remainder of my life. To take away the occasions pretended for all differences between us, clear yourself, if you please, of all which has been reported of you concerning my actions; review the depositions of the strangers taken in Ireland; let those of the Jesuits last executed be represented to you; give liberty to those who would undertake to charge me publickly, and permit me to enter upon my defence; if any evil be found in me, let me suffer it, it shall be patiently when I shall know the occasion of it; if any good, suffer me not to be worst treated for it, with your very great commission before God and man.

"The vilest criminals that are in your prisons, born under your obedience, are admitted to their justification; and their accusers, and their accusations, are always declared to them. Why, then, shall not the same order have place towards me, a Sovereign Queen, your nearest relation and lawful heir? I think that this last circumstance has hitherto been, on the side of my enemies, the principal cause of it, and of all their calumnies, to make their unjust pretences slide between the two, by keeping us in division. But, alas, they have now little reason and less need to torment me more upon this account. For I protest to you upon mine honour that I look this day for no kingdom but that of my God; whom I see preparing me for the better conclusion of all my afflictions and adversities past."

Reverting to the injustices to which her son was then subjected by traitors in Scotland, she exhorts Elizabeth not to give countenance to their actions, and proceeds in the following amazingly naive manner:--

"I shall be contented then, only at your not permitting my son to receive any injury from this country (which is all that I have ever required of you before, even when an army was sent to the borders to prevent justice from being done to that detestable Morton), and that none of your subjects directly or indirectly intermeddle any more in the affairs of Scotland, unless it is with my knowledge, to whom all cognizance of these things belongs, or with the assistance of some one on the part of the most Christian King, my good brother; whom, as our principal ally, I desire to make privy to the whole of this cause, because of the little credit that he can have with the traitors who detain my son at present.

"But, Madam, with all this freedom of speech, which, I foresee will in some sort displease you, though it be the truth itself, you will find it more strange, I assure myself, that I come now to importune you again with a request of much greater importance, and yet very easy for you to grant, and release to me. This is, that having not been able hitherto, by accommodating myself patiently so long a time to the rigorous treatment of this captivity, and carrying myself sincerely in all things, yea, even to the last, that could concern you a very little, to gain myself some assurance of my entire affection towards you; all my hope being taken away by it of being better treated for the very short time which remains to me of life; I supplicate you, by the honour of the sorrowful passion of our Saviour and Redeemer, Jesus Christ, again I supplicate you, at once to permit me to withdraw myself out of your realm, into some place of repose, to search out some comfort for my poor body, so wearied as it is with continual sorrow, and with liberty of my conscience to prepare my soul for God, who is calling for it daily."

* * * * *

"Your prison, without any right or foundation, has already destroyed my body, of which you will shortly have the end, if it continues there a little longer; and my enemies will not have much time for glutting their cruelties on me; nothing remains of me but the soul, which all your power cannot make captive. Give it, then, room for aspiring a little more freely after its salvation, which alone it seeks for at this day, more than any grandeur of this world. It seems to me that it cannot be to you any great satisfaction, honour, and advantage, for mine enemies to trample my life under foot, till they have stifled me in your presence. Whereas, if in this extremity, however late it be, you release me out of their hands, you will bind me greatly to you, and bind all those who belong to me, particularly my poor child, whom you will, perhaps, make sure to yourself by it.

"Two things I have principally to require at the close; the one that, near as I am to going out of this world, I may have with me, for my consolation, some honourable church-man, to remind me daily of the course which I have to finish, and teach me how to complete it according to my religion in which I am firmly resolved to live and die.

"This is a last duty which cannot be denied to the most mean and miserable person that lives; it is a liberty which you grant to all foreign embassadours; as also all other Catholick kings give to your embassadours the exercise of their religion. And even I myself have not hitherto forced my own subjects to anything contrary to their religion, though I had all power and authority over them. And that I in this extremity should be deprived of such freedom, you cannot, with justice, require. What advantage will redound to you, when you shall deny it to me? I hope God will excuse me if, oppressed by you in this manner, I do not render to him any duty but what I shall be permitted to do in my heart. But you will set a very bad example to the other Princes of Christendom, to act towards their subjects with the same rigour that you shall show to me, a Sovereign Queen, and your nearest relation; which I am, and will be as long as I live, in despite of mine enemies."

Here she enters upon a justification of her conduct in view of a charge which had been brought against her, namely, that contrary to her promise, and without the knowledge of Elizabeth, she had entered into certain political negotiations with her son in Scotland. She reviews the circumstances of the case, indicates her own and Elizabeth's respective practices, and then refers to her cousin's consideration "which of us has proceeded with the greatest sincerity." Finally she closes her lengthy letter with the following appeal:--

"Resume the ancient pledges of your good nature; bind your relations to yourself; give me the satisfaction before I die that, seeing all matters happily settled again between us, my soul, when delivered from this body, may not be constrained to display its lamentations before God for the wrong which you have suffered to be done me here below; but, rather, that being happily united to you, it may quit this captivity to set forward towards him, whom I pray to inspire you happily upon my very just and more than reasonable complaints and grievances.

"At Sheffield, this 8th of November, one thousand five hundred and eighty-two.

"Your very disconsolate, nearest relation, and affectionate cousin,

"MARIE E."

But no appeal, however deeply it might possibly touch the heart of the Tudor Queen, could turn her from that one purpose which, in her ever-changing policy, remained forever fixed, of preventing the possibility of Mary's returning to public life. With all her unwomanly qualities, however, it cannot be presumed that she was always insensible to the pathos of her captive's language, or even to the better impulses of her own heart. She was not, as certain tyrants seem to have been, cruel from the mere love of inflicting pain. The fierce outbursts of anger and the arbitrary commands with which she overawed Parliament when other means of carrying her point failed, did not prevent her from being sincerely interested in procuring the happiness of her people; and it is not wholly without cause that she has received, from a portion of her subjects, the title of "Good Queen Bess." But woe to him who stood between her and her interest. Her ambition would not be thwarted by any inconvenient delicacy or dictate of conscience. Whether in her more peaceful hours she practised "modest stillness and humility," is irrelevant to the present question; it is beyond doubt however, that when the blast of jealousy, suspicion, or hatred, blew in her ears she knew how to "imitate the action of the tiger." It must in truth be admitted that her position in relation to the Scottish Queen, was a difficult one; but it should, in equal truth, be admitted that her own dishonesty was cause of the most part of her trouble. To have within her realm the one whom a large portion of her subjects considered by right Queen of England, and through whom the Pope and the Catholic powers hoped to see the island restored to the obedience of the Holy See, was eminently calculated to make her life uncomfortable. She was conscious that she was an object of hatred to many who had power to do her no end of mischief. But she must have foreseen these troubles when she elected to detain Mary a prisoner. At any rate she must soon have learned that so long as she chose to be the jailer of the most beautiful, accomplished and renowned woman in Europe, she could not hope for a peaceful career. Who so foolish as to think that Mary would not use all her energy to regain her liberty, or that powerful parties at home and abroad would not make the captive's cause their own? Certainly not the crafty Elizabeth. Yet a simple act of justice--the release of the prisoner whom she unjustly and ungenerously detained--would have removed the cause of half her anxieties. Elizabeth's troubles, therefore, were voluntarily assumed, and were part of the price which she was content to pay for the gratification of having in her power the woman and queen whose superior beauty, and title to the throne of England, had long before aroused her undying hatred. It is childish and ridiculous for historians to excuse Elizabeth's harshness on the plea that Mary's plotting and intriguing rendered severe treatment necessary. The same argument would justify the bandit in maltreating his victim who would be so ungrateful as to attempt escaping from his custody.

CHAPTER XI.

THE BEGINNING OF THE END.

The spacious park of Sheffield, in which Mary's prison was situated, beautiful as was the natural scenery of river, mountain and cultivated slope, that extended far beyond it, could offer no antidote to the "*dura catena, et misera paena,*" in which she languished. Her mind had already been stored with pictures of the choicest rural scenery in France, and of the rugged grandeur of Aberdeen and Perthshire; and the variegated charms on which she could now gaze from her prison window only served to produce that sad pleasure which we feel in renewing memories of joys that have forever departed. Well, has Mr. Samuel Roberts (in his feeling lines in reference to her stay at Sheffield Lodge) presumed that she gazed upon the "lovely scene" "through tears":--

Alone, here oft may Scotia's beauteous queen,

Through tears have gazed upon the lovely scene,

Victim of villainy, of woman's hate,

Of fiery zeal, of wiles and storms of state;

Torn from her throne, her country and her child,

And cast an exiled monarch in this wild,

She here was taught, what youthful beauty ne'er

While seated on a throne, had deigned to hear,

To say submissive, at the closing scene,

"'Tis well that I have thus afflicted been;"

Then calmly on the block, in faith, resign

Three heart-corrupting crowns, for one divine.

Reader,--the ways of God are not like thine.

In August, 1584, Shrewsbury was released of his charge. He had served long and faithfully in a capacity that was repulsive to his instincts; and after fifteen full years of close acquaintance with the captive Queen, he was able to assure Elizabeth "that if the Queen of Scotland promise anything she will not break her word."

With the withdrawal of Shrewsbury, a new and more ominous period opened in the life of the Scottish Queen. She was removed from Sheffield to Wingfield; and again from Wingfield to Tutbury. Here, in April, 1585, she was committed to the charge of that "narrow, boorish and bitter secretary," Sir Amias Paulet, who seems to have been selected mainly with a view of driving her to desperation and of rendering the last days of her life as bitter and insufferable as possible. Shrewsbury had, it is true, executed the commands of his mistress; but he had done so without making it clear that he found pleasure in being the instrument of tyranny. In the meantime his upright, gentlemanly character modified, as far as was consistent with his duty and safety, the rigour which it was his office to enforce. Paulet, on the contrary, carried into effect the will of Elizabeth to the letter, and in addition satiated his own fierce and fanatical hatred of his helpless prisoner. What wonder if Mary should become desperate and resolve to embark on whatever expedition, daring and reckless though it might be, that gave even a probable hope of securing her liberty? Seventeen years of waiting and negotiating for a peaceable settlement of her case, had resulted in failure; nay, had left her in greater distress than ever. Whatever quota of humanity had tempered the severity of her treatment, was now replaced by the studied rudeness of her keeper; her son had just disassociated completely his political interests from hers; and the movements and tactics of her enemies awakened and intensified her old fear that she should soon be visited with a secret and unnatural death.

The defection of James deeply wounded the mother's heart. "This was the most unkindest cut of all." That the one for whom she had so long defended the independence of Scotland against the English claim of suzerainty; that the one from whom she had hopefully waited through years of patient suffering to receive even one word that would assure her that she had a son growing up to love and assist her; that the one whom she remembered only as an innocent and playful infant, from whom she had been, torn away by heartless traitors,--that he should abandon her when fresh miseries were gathering thick and fast around her, was more than she could calmly suffer, and for a short time her wounded love and feelings of indignation were revealed in sad and bitter complaint. "Was it for this," she wrote to the French Ambassador, "that I have endured so much, in order to preserve for him the inheritance to which I have a just right? I am far from envying his authority in Scotland. I desire no power, nor wish to set my foot in that kingdom, if it were not for the pleasure of once embracing a son, whom I have hitherto loved with too tender affection. Whatever he either enjoys or expects, he derived it from me. From him I never received assistance, supply or benefit of any kind. Let not my allies treat him any longer as a king; he holds that dignity by my consent; and if a speedy repentance does not appease my just resentment, I will load him with a parent's curse, and surrender my crown, with all its pretensions, to one who will receive them with gratitude, and defend them with vigour."

The English Parliament had recently framed a statute, out of special consideration for the Queen of Scots, by which it was enacted that, not only the person *by* whom, but also the person *for* whom, a rebellion should be excited against the majesty of Elizabeth, might be visited with several penalties, and "pursued to death," and it only remained to induce Mary to avail herself of the benefits of that benign legislation.[#] The event long hoped for by her enemies ere long came to pass. The net of Secretary Walsingham's cunning intrigue gradually involved the unsuspecting victim in its deadly meshes. In April, 1586, a young English Catholic gentleman, named Babington, whom a spirit of chivalry had deeply interested in the Scottish Queen's behalf, and who was stung to desperation by the injustices which he and his co-religionists were obliged to suffer because they would not forswear the faith of their English forefathers, was drawn into a plot, devised by Morgan and Paget in France, for the overthrow of Elizabeth and the liberation of Mary. This plot is known in English history as the Babington plot, though it might, with far more truth, be called the Walsingham plot. Walsingham was aware of its existence for some months before the services of Babington were solicited. His agents, especially Pooley and Gilbert Gifford, combined the offices of staunch conspirators and spies at the same time, and kept their master fully informed of what was being done. The assassination of Elizabeth formed no part of the original design. It was only at a consultation, held at Paris, in April, in which Gifford took an active part, that this daring project was agreed upon, and that it was resolved to seek the aid of the unfortunate young Babington. In the meantime, Walsingham, anxious that Mary might be entangled as completely as possible in his net, and tempted to ratify the compromising scheme that he himself, through his worthy agent, had helped to concoct, arranged that she should be given favourable opportunities for communication with her outside friends; but he equally provided that the medium of communication should be persons in his own service. Thus, the letters she sent out, as well as those she received, all passed through the office of the Secretary of State, were deciphered there by another noted instrument of the Secretary's, named Philipps, and forwarded to their destination with whatever addition or interpolation seemed best calculated to provoke a reply directly implicating the unsuspecting captive.

[#] In justice it must be stated, that it was not under this statute, but under a later one requiring the complicity of the party in whose interest the treasonable measures should be taken, that the Queen of Scots was subsequently condemned.

Elizabeth and her Minister knew that the plot had now reached a point beyond which it would be perilous to allow it to proceed. Early in August, Babington and his associates were arrested, and on the 16th of the same month Mary, who was then at Chartley, in Staffordshire, was removed without forewarning, her two Secretaries, Curle and Nau being separated from her, and all her papers seized; a few weeks later (25th September) she was lodged in the ominous castle of Fotheringay, in Northamptonshire.

"The name of Fotheringay had been connected through a long course of years with many sorrows and much crime, and during the last three years the castle had been used as a state prison. Catherine of Arragon, more fortunate than her great-niece, had flatly refused to be imprisoned within its walls, declaring that 'to Fotheringay she would not go, unless bound with cart rope and dragged thither.' Tradition, often kinder than history, asserts that James VI., after his accession to the English throne, destroyed the castle; and though it is no longer possible to credit him with this act of filial love or remorse, time has obliterated almost every trace of the once grim fortress. A green mound, an isolated mass of masonry, and a few thistles, are all that now remain to mark the scene of Mary's last sufferings. Very different was the aspect of Fotheringay at the time of which we write. Then, protected by its double moat, it frowned on the surrounding country in almost impregnable strength. The front of the castle and the great gateway faced the north, while to the southwest rose the keep. A large courtyard occupied the interior of the building, in which were situated the chief apartments, including the chapel and the great hall destined to be the scene of the queen's death."[#]

[#] Hon. Mrs. Maxwell Scott in "*The Tragedy of Fotheringay.*"

A moment had now arrived in which the helpless Queen, broken down by nineteen years of close confinement and consequent ill-health, had heed to summon up all her native courage. Her papers and most of her private correspondence had been carried off to London; her Secretaries, who had been privy to all her plots and plans, had been separated from her, and with the terrors of the rack before their minds would be forced not only to divulge what they knew, but still worse to subscribe, perhaps, to what they did not believe; and she, without counsel or comfort, was left in the hands of her enemies. The manoeuvrings of her enemies at this time show that they expected that, finding herself alone and in the extremity of danger, she would cast herself at the feet of Elizabeth, confess that she was guilty, and sue for pardon. But they had yet to learn the calm dignity, the unflinching courage and the Christian hopefulness with which Mary Stewart could place her neck upon the block.

A commission of the nobles was appointed to try her at Fotheringay, on the charge of plotting against the life of Elizabeth. Mary protested against the manner in which she was to be tried as belittling an independent sovereign, who was subject neither to the laws nor to the Queen of England. But at length, through fear that her refusal to appear before the commissioners would be interpreted as a sign of guilt, and through dread of being dispatched secretly by poison--in which case her enemies could assert what they wished about the way she died--she consented to appear, and for two days sat before the commissioners listening to and answering accusations.

The proceedings in which she was constrained to take part cannot properly be called a trial. She was deprived, as far as possible, of every means of defence; she had no secretary, her correspondence was withheld from her, she was refused counsel. "Alas," she said to her faithful servant Melville, as she took her seat the first day before the Commissioners, "Alas, here are many counsellors, but not one for me." Nevertheless she spoke with so much courage and energy, and showed so little regard for the wrath of her enemies, or even for death itself, so long as her honour was vindicated, that she surprised and partly confounded the hard-hearted zealots who were hounding her to death.

On the 14th of October, the trial was opened in a large room in Fotheringay Castle. Seated on benches placed in the middle of the room and along both walls were all the Peers of England who could conveniently be brought together, as well as the various officers of the court. Once upon a time, in the brave days of knight-errantry, no injured lady need have feared to present herself and plead her cause before the assembled chivalry of "Merry England," but 'old times were changed, old manners gone.' At 9 o'clock in the forenoon, the Queen entered, supported by Melville and Bourgoin her physician. She had been personally acquainted with but very few of those who sat there to pass judgment upon her. Many of them had been known to her by name, a few had been attached to her cause, and she looked about in the hope of meeting an eye that would reveal the presence of a friend. But she was disappointed. No one in that hostile assembly, however he might feel in his heart, would venture now to betray any sign of sympathy. Three faces must have impressed her more than all the rest as suggesting, in three different periods, the history of her troubled career. There she saw Sir Ralph Sadler, the English Ambassador who, forty-four years before, had stood over her cradle in the nursery at Linlithgow and pronounced her a "right fair and goodly child;" there she saw Sir William Cecil (now Lord Burleigh), who had been her ablest and most industrious enemy through all the years of her short reign, and who had contributed more perhaps that any other individual to produce the Scottish anarchy in which she had lost her crown; and there she met, for the first time, the gaze of the crafty and vigilant Sir Francis Walsingham, whose mephistophelian devices had led her to the precipice over which she now hung, without an arm to save her.

CHAPTER XII.

THE EVIDENCE AGAINST THE QUEEN OF SCOTS.

Replying to the accusations brought against her, Mary did not deny that, having given up hope of being liberated by Elizabeth, she had treated with foreign powers for her deliverance; but she protested that she had never consented to the assassination of Elizabeth, and that she would rather remain all her life in prison than stain her conscience with that crime. Nor can I see that any evidence had been produced to prove that she did. Her intercepted letter in reply to Babington, in which she was said to have sanctioned the projected murder of Elizabeth, was not exhibited at the trial. Here we find the same shuffling as in the case of the Casket Letters. If her accusers had decisive proof of her guilt, why did they not give her a fair trial, and employ those means which would make her guilt evident? Babington, instead of being kept as a witness, was put to death. Her two secretaries, who had been terrified into testifying to something,--what exactly they did testify we cannot be certain,--were kept out of the way, and never confronted with their mistress. Her letter on which the case depended had been written in cipher; yet the original in cipher was shown neither to her secretaries nor to herself, but only what was passed off as a translation of it into French. But what need of this traffic in second-hand documents, if the original, which would settle all dispute, could be safely exposed to the light of investigation? Neither the strained dialectics of a Hume, nor the brilliant rhetoric of a Froude, can avail against the force of argument springing from Walsingham's determination not to exhibit the original documents. Mary had been charged with being party to a plot for the murder of Elizabeth, and her correspondence with Babington was made the basis of evidence against her. Hence common justice demanded that the correspondence should be taken, as far as possible, at first hand. Yet, Walsingham and Philipps, although they had in their possession, at least, a minute in Mary's own hand of her last answer to Babington and the same cast into the form of a letter in French by Nau, made use of what they alleged was a copy of that incriminating answer. Mary denied that she had ever dictated the words of Philipps' decipher in reference to the murder of Elizabeth. Philipps, the associate of Walsingham, and the bitter enemy of Mary, went sponsor for the correctness of the decipher. The trial therefore was reduced to a contest between the veracity of Mary and the veracity of Philipps. It is hardly to be doubted that, guilty or not guilty, Mary would have disowned the authorship of the compromising clauses. But if her denial was worthless as evidence of her innocence, the assertion of a forger in the employ of her enemies was likewise worthless as evidence of her guilt. Why, then, were not the original papers laid before the commissioners, that she might be reduced to silence by the evidence of her own and of her secretary's handwriting? Shall we be asked to believe that Walsingham, if he had all he needed in the original, would have had recourse to a copy? Indeed, Mary's letter, as it has reached us through Philipps and Walsingham, presents an incoherence of parts which, even if every other reason were wanting, would render its genuineness extremely doubtful. The argument founded on this incoherence has been frequently used, but its strength remains unimpaired. Mary orders that nothing shall be done towards releasing her from prison until Elizabeth is murdered. Four horsemen are to be kept in readiness to immediately inform her that this has been accomplished. Then she is to be set at liberty, but care must be taken that the army prepared to receive her, or the stronghold destined to shelter her, be such as will render her person secure, for (she writes) "it were sufficient excuse given to that queen in catching me again, to enclose me in some hold, out of which I should never escape, if she did use me no worse." This precaution against the revenge of Elizabeth is quite natural, and just what we should expect from Mary in her letter to Babington; but it would be inconceivable and absurd if Mary had already made provision that Elizabeth should first of all be murdered. Had Philipps forged the entire letter, he would not have committed this blunder, but even an expert may reveal his identity when he attempts to interpolate a lengthy document.

It will avail but little to insist that there remains what Froude calls the "positive proof of two very credible witnesses" in support of the charge against the Scottish queen. These "very credible witnesses" were Mary's secretaries, Nau and Curle; and the "positive proof" was their subscription to a "copy"--that ever recurring "copy"--of Mary's deciphered answer to Babington's last letter, which had been wrung from them in circumstances little calculated to enhance its value.

Since their forced separation from Mary at Chartley, they had been carefully guarded and accurately learned the nature of the evidence which they were expected to give. On the 20th. September, Babington and six of his associates were made a ghastly and terrifying spectacle to every weak-hearted friend of Mary's. "They were all hanged but for a moment, according to the letter of the sentence, taken down while the susceptibility of agony was unimpaired, and cut in pieces afterwards, with due precautions for the protraction of pain."[#]

[#] Froude, "History of England," Vol. XII., Chap. 69.

The third day following, while this ominous lesson of vengeance was fresh in every mind, the two secretaries were forced to ratify by their oath the testimony which they had already given (Sept. 5th) to the correctness of the "copy." The testimony which they now ratified had been appended to the copy in these words:--"*Telle ou semblable me semble avoir esté la reponse escripte en francoys par monsieur Nau, laquelle J'ay traduict et mis en chiffre.--Gilbert Curle."* "*Je pense de vray que c'est la lettre escripte par sa Majesté à Babington, come il me souvient.--Nau."* "This letter or one like it appears to me to have been the answer written in French by monsieur Nau, which I translated and put into cipher.--Gilbert Curle."

"I think in truth that this is the letter written by Her Majesty to Babington, *as far as I can remember.*--Nau."

These equivocal testimonies contain the force of all the evidence produced against Mary. It is unnecessary to point out the impossibility of resting a conviction upon them. That is clear to every intelligent reader acquainted with the circumstances in which they were obtained and with the history of the prosecution as already summarily indicated, up to this point. The phrases "*this or one like it,*" "*as well as I can remember,*" insignificant as they might seem if employed in the absence of compulsion, will in their present connection strike every reflecting mind as the feeble devices of men striving to hold a safe course between the Scylla and the Charibdis of perjury and the rack.

Whether Mary would or would not accept an offer of deliverance that involved the life of Elizabeth, is a purely speculative question, which does not affect the nature of the evidence produced against her. This, however, may be observed, that nearly four years earlier, when a conspiracy similar to the Babington plot against the life of Elizabeth was being organized by some of her friends on the Continent, she, on being acquainted of it, "refused," (so wrote the Papal Nuncio at Paris to the Cardinal of Como), "to listen to it." But, when hope in Elizabeth's good intentions completely failed, and increased rigour deepened the misery of her prison-life, reasons which had hitherto seemed inadequate might now convince her that she was not obliged to live with the axe of the executioner or the dagger of the assassin, raised over her head because liberty could be brought to her only through the blood of her jailer.

CHAPTER XIII.

EXTRACTS FROM HER ADDRESSES TO THE COMMISSIONERS.

Every word and act of this unhappy Princess, more especially as her life neared its close, have proved so interesting to students of her history, that I have deemed it well to reproduce here some of her speeches and utterances before the Commissioners appointed to try her.

On the first day of the trial, the Lord Chancellor, Bromley, having signified the causes which had impelled Elizabeth to take action against her as the disturber of religion and the public peace, Mary replied as follows:--

"I came into this kingdom under promise of assistance and aid against my enemies, and not as a subject, as I could prove to you had I my papers; instead of which I have been detained and imprisoned. I protest publicly that I am an independent sovereign and princess, and I recognize no superior but God alone. I therefore require that before I proceed further, it be recorded that whatever I may say in replying here to the Commissioners of my good sister, the Queen of England (who, I consider, has been wrongly and falsely prejudiced against me), shall not be to my prejudice, nor that of the princes, my allies, nor the king, my son, or any of those who may succeed me. I make this protestation not out of regard to my life, or in order to conceal the truth, but purely for the preservation of the honour and dignity of my royal prerogative, and to show that in consenting to appear before this commission I do so, not as a subject to Queen Elizabeth, but only from my desire to clear myself, and to show to all the world that I am not guilty of this crime against the person of the Queen, with which it seems I am charged. I wish to reply to this point alone, I desire this protest to be publicly recorded, and I appeal to all the lords and nobles present to bear me testimony should it one day be necessary."

In the course of the afternoon discussion, she made bitter complaint of the unfair treatment to which she had been subjected:--

"I have, as you see, lost my health and the use of my limbs. I cannot walk without assistance, nor use my arms, and I spend most of my time confined to bed by sickness. Not only this, but through my trials, I have lost the small intellectual gifts bestowed on me by God, such as my memory, which would have aided me to recall those things which I have seen and read, and which might be useful to me in the cruel position in which I now find myself ... Not content with this, my enemies now endeavour to complete my ruin, using against me means that are unheard of towards persons of my rank, and unknown in this kingdom before the reign of the present Queen, and even now not approved by rightful judges, but only by unlawful authority. Against these I appeal to Almighty God, to all Christian princes, and to the estates of this kingdom duly and lawfully assembled. Being innocent and falsely suspected, I am ready to maintain and defend my honour, provided that my defence be publicly recorded, and that I make it in the presences of some princes or foreign judges, or even before my natural judges; and this without prejudice to my mother the Church, to kings, sovereign princes and to my son. With regard to the pretensions long put forward by the English (as their chronicles testify) to suzerainty over my predecessors, the Kings of Scotland, I utterly deny and protest against them, and will not, like a *femme-de peu de coeur*, admit them, nor by any present act, to which I may be constrained, will I fortify such a claim, whereby I should dishonour those princes, my ancestors, and acknowledge them to have been traitors and rebels. Rather than do this, I am ready to die for God and my rights in this quarrel, in which, as in all others, I am innocent."

Burleigh had reproached her with having assumed the arms of England, and a spirited discussion after a somewhat legal fashion followed. Passing with characteristic facility from that unprofitable topic, Mary proceeded in the following spirited and pathetic manner:--

"God and you know whether I have a right or not to the crown of England. I have offered myself to maintain the rights of my sister, Queen Elizabeth, as being the eldest, but I have no scruple of conscience in desiring the second rank, as being the legitimate and nearest heir. I am the daughter of James V., king of Scotland, and grand-daughter of Henry VII. This cannot be taken from me by any law, or council or assembly, or judgment, nor consequently can my rights. I know well that my enemies and those who wish to deprive me of those rights have done up till now all that they can to injure me, and have essayed all illegitimate means, even to attempting my life, as is well known, and has been discovered in certain places and by certain persons whom I could name, were it necessary; but God, who is the best Judge, and who never forgets His own, has until now, in His infinite mercy and goodness, preserved me from all dangers, and I hope that he will continue to do so and will not abandon me, knowing that He is all truth, and that He has promised not to abandon His servants in their need. He has extended His hand over me to afflict me, but He has given me this grace of patience to bear the adversities which it has pleased Him to send me. I do not desire vengeance. I leave it to Him who is the just Avenger of the innocent and of those who suffer for His name, under whose power and will I take shelter. I prefer the conduct of Esther to that of Judith, although both are approved by the Church. I pray God to do with me according to His good pleasure, to His praise and honour, and to the greater glory of His Church, in which I wish to live and die, in which I have been brought up and educated, and for which (as I have already protested several times), I would shed my blood to the last drop, being resolved to suffer all that God wishes. I do not fear the menaces of men. I will never deny Jesus Christ, knowing well that those who deny Him in this world, He will deny before His Father. I demand another hearing, and that I be allowed an advocate to plead my cause, or that I be believed on the word of a Queen.... I came to England relying on the friendship and promises of your Queen. Look here, my Lords, [at this point she took a ring from her finger], see this pledge of love and protection which I received from your mistress, regard it well. Trusting to this pledge, I came amongst you. You all know how it has been kept."

Her criticism of the second-hand evidence, secured from her secretaries in her absence, is so just that I cannot pass it over without giving, at least, some extracts from it. It will be observed, that while sharing in the suspicion not uncommon at the time, that Nau had betrayed her to save himself, her fairmindedness and charitable disposition prevented her from condemning him without a hearing.

"Why," she asked, "are not Nau and Curle examined in my presence? They at any rate are still alive. If my enemies were assured that they would confirm their pretended avowals, they would be here without doubt. If they have written, be it what it may, concerning the enterprise, they have done it of themselves, and did not communicate it to me, and on this point I disavow them." ......

"I know well that Nau had many peculiarities, likings and intentions, that I cannot mention, in public, but which I much regret, for he does me great injustice. For my part, I do not wish to accuse my secretaries, but I plainly see that what they have said is from fear of torture and death. Under promises of their lives, and in order to save themselves, they have excused themselves at my expense, fancying that I could thereby more easily save myself; at the same time not knowing where I was and not suspecting the manner in which I am treated ... As to Curle, if he has done anything suspicious, he has been compelled to do it by Nau, whom he feared much to displease.... *And yet I do not think that either the one or the other would have forgotten himself so far.*"

"I commanded him (Nau) it is true, and in a general way supported his doings, as all princes are accustomed to do, but it is for him to answer for his private doings. I cannot but think he has been acting under constraint in this matter. Feeling himself to be feeble and weak by nature, and fearing torture, he thought to escape by throwing all the blame on me."

*   *   *   *   *

"I dictated nothing to them (the secretaries) but what nature herself inspired me, for the recovery at least of my liberty. I can only be convicted by my words or by my own writings. If, without my consent, but have written something to the prejudice of the Queen, your mistress, let them suffer the punishment of their rashness. *But of this I am very sure, if they were now in my presence, they would clear me on the spot of all blame, and would put me out of case.* Show me, at least, the minutes of my correspondence written by myself; they will bear witness to what I now assert."

On the morning of the second day, Mary made a strong and dignified protest against the manner in which the trial had been conducted, and after specifying the treatment she expected to receive when she consented to appear before the Commissioners, proceeded:--

"Instead of this, I find myself overwhelmed under the importunity of a crowd of advocates and lawyers, who appear to be more versed in the formalities of petty courts of justice, in little towns, than in the investigation of questions such as the present. And although I was promised that I should be simply questioned and examined on one point,--that, namely, concerning the attempt on the person of the Queen,--they have presumed to accuse me, each striving who should surpass the other in stating and exaggerating facts, and attempting to force me to reply to questions which I do not understand, and which have nothing to do with the Commission. Is it not an unworthy act to submit to such conduct of such people, the title of a princess, one little accustomed to such procedures and formalities? And is it not against all right, justice and reason to deliver her over to them, weak and ill as she is, and deprived of counsel, without papers or notes or secretary? It is very easy for many together, and, as it appears to me, conspiring for the same object, to vanquish by force of words a solitary and defenceless woman. There is not one, I think, among you, let him be the cleverest man you will, who would be capable of resisting or defending himself, were he in my place. I am alone, taken by surprise, and forced to reply to so many people who are unfriendly to me, and who have long been preparing for this occasion; and who appear to be more influenced by vehement prejudice and anger, than by a desire of discovering the truth and fulfilling the duties laid down for them by the Commission."

Referring to the complaint that, in Rome, public prayers had been offered for her, under the title of Queen of England, she remarked:--"If the Pope gives me the title of Queen, it is not for me to correct him. He knows what he does much better than I do. I thank him, all Christian people and all Catholic nations for the prayers they daily offer for me, and I pray them to continue to do so, and to remember me in their Masses."

As regards her attitude towards her Protestant subjects she said:--"You know very well that in my own kingdom I never interfered with any of the Protestants, but, on the contrary, tried to win them always by gentleness and clemency, which I carried too far, and for which I have been blamed. It has been the cause of my ruin, for my subjects became proud and haughty, and abused my clemency; indeed, they now complain that they were never so well off as under my government."

The trial ended on the 15th October. Mary rose from her seat before the Commissioners and passed out of the hall, addressing a few words of good-humoured reproach to the lawyers for their "quibbling," as she moved past the table around which they were seated. The Commissioners, in compliance with instructions received from Elizabeth, withdrew to Westminster before passing sentence. Assembled in the Star-Chamber ten days later, they declared Mary "to be accessory to Babington's conspiracy, and to have imagined diverse matters, tending to the hurt, death, and destruction of Elizabeth, contrary to the express words of the statute, made for the security of the Queen's life" (Camden). Parliament sat a few days after, and both houses, having sanctioned the sentence of the Commissioners, presented an address to Elizabeth, requesting her to publish and execute without delay the sentence against her dangerous rival.

Mary in the meantime was ignorant of what was being done since the rising of the Commission at Fotheringay. However, she maintained an extraordinary cheerfulness and surprised the observant Sir Amias by her "quietness and serenity." The feast of All Saints arrived, but without the joyous anthems and splendid ceremonial that marked it in Catholic lands. The Queen passed the day reading the lives of the Saints and Martyrs and praying in her oratory. In the afternoon she received a visit from Paulet. In the course of their conversation, this censorious pedant, anxious to execute the will of Elizabeth, who had instructed him to carefully observe whether his prisoner should reveal a disposition to sue for pardon, undertook to instruct her in the necessity of having a clear conscience and of confessing her crimes before God and the world. Mary promptly answered, saying:-- "No one can say that he is free from sin. I am a woman and human, and have offended God, and I repent of my sins, and pray God to forgive me, doing penance for the same; but at present I do not know to whom I could or should confess--God forbid that I should ask you to be my confessor."

CHAPTER XIV.

THE SENTENCE OF DEATH.

On November the 30th, 1586, Lord Buckhurst, as envoy of Queen Elizabeth, waited upon the lonely captive, and announced to her that sentence of death had been passed upon her. "The person of the Queen," added Buckhurst, "the state and religion are no longer safe; it is impossible for you both to live, and therefore one must die. For this end then, in order that you should not be taken by surprise, Mr. Beale and I have been sent to warn you to prepare for death, and we will send you the Bishop of Peterborough or the Dean of ---- for your consolation."

The news was, in some respects a relief to Mary; it relaxed her consuming mental tension. Now she knew the worst, and her conduct needed no longer to be disturbed by alternating hopes and fears. She had striven hard, during the weary years of her captivity, to resign herself with Christian cheerfulness to the inevitable. But the love of liberty, and perhaps too a subtle desire of revenge, had at times ruffled the serenity of her spirit, and had dulled the pure flame of her religious zeal. Human aid now seemed no longer available, human prospects of glory and power no longer captivated her imagination, and the time and energy which she had hitherto expended on profitless plans and visionary deeds, she could now devote, with rich and enduring profit, to the preparation for a better life. When she heard Lord Buckhurst's message, her face, as Camden relates, "became illumined with an extraordinary joy at the thought that she was about to die for the cause of religion," and with perfect composure, she made answer:--"I expected nothing else. This is the manner in which you generally proceed with regard to persons of my quality, and who are nearly related to the crown, so that none may live who aspire to it. For long I have known that you would bring me to this in the end. I have loved the queen and the country, and have done all that I could for the preservation of both. The offers which I have made are the proof of this, as Beale can bear me witness. I do not fear death, and shall suffer it with a good heart. I have never been the author of any conspiracy to injure the queen. I have several times been offered my freedom, and have been blamed for refusing my consent. My partizans have abandoned me and troubled themselves no more with my affairs. To prevent this I have attempted to obtain my deliverance by gentle means, to my great disadvantage, till at last, being repulsed on the one side and pressed on the other, I placed myself in the hands of my friends, and have taken part with Christian and Catholic princes, not, as I have before declared, and as the English themselves can bear witness by the papers which they have in their possession, through ambition nor the desire of a greater position, but I have done it for the honour of God and His Church, and for my deliverance from the state of captivity and misery in which I am placed. I am a Catholic,--of a different religion from yourselves; and for this reason you will take care not to let me live. I am grieved that my death cannot be of as much benefit to the kingdom as I fear it will do it harm; and this I say not from any ill-feeling or from any desire to live. For my part, I am weary of being in this world, nor do I, or any one else, profit by my being here. But I look forward to a better life, and I thank God for giving me this grace of dying in his quarrel. No greater good can come to me in this world; it is what I have most begged of God and most wished for, as being the thing most honourable for myself and most profitable for the salvation of my soul. I have never had the intention of changing my religion for any earthly kingdom, or grandeur, or good whatever, nor of denying Jesus Christ or His name, nor will I now. You may feel well assured that I shall die in this entire faith and with my good will, and as happy in doing so as I was ever for anything that has come to me in my life. I pray God to have mercy on the poor Catholics of this kingdom, who are persecuted and oppressed for their religion. The only thing I regret is, that it has not pleased God to give me before I die the grace to see them, able to live in full liberty of conscience in the faith of their parents, in the Catholic Church, and serving God as they desire to do. I am not ignorant that for long certain persons have been plotting against me; and to speak plainly, I know well it has been done at the instance of one who professes to be my enemy. But I have spoken sufficiently of this before the Commissioners."

After this trying ordeal, Mary's first thought was to send letters of final greeting to her dearest friends. She wrote to the Archbishop of Glasgow, then in Paris; to Pope Sixtus V., to Barnard De Mendoça, Spanish Ambassador at Paris; and to the Duke of Guise. In the course of her letter to the Archbishop, referring to the proposal that she should accept the services of the Anglican divines, she writes:--

"As to their bishops, I praise God that without their aid I know well enough my offences against God and His Church, and that I do not approve their errors, nor wish to communicate with them in any way. But if it pleased them to permit me to have a Catholic priest, I said I would accept that very willingly, and even demanded it in the name of Jesus Christ, in order to dispose my conscience, and to participate in the Holy Sacraments, on leaving this world. They answered me that, do what I would, I should not be either saint or martyr, as I was to die for the murder of their queen and for wishing to dispossess her. I replied that I was not so presumptuous as to aspire to these two honours; but that although they had power over my body by divine permission, not by justice, as I am a sovereign queen, as I have always protested, still they had not power over my soul, nor could they prevent me from hoping that, through the mercy of God, who died for me, he will accept from me my blood and my life which I offer to Him for the maintenance of His Church outside of which I should never desire to rule any worldly kingdom."

Her letter to the Pope is lengthy, but as no one interested in her history would be satisfied with an abbreviated form of so interesting a document, I shall give it in full.

"Jesus Maria,

"Holy Father,--As it has pleased God by His divine providence so to ordain, that in His Church, under His Son, Jesus Christ crucified, all those who should believe in Him and be baptized in the name of the Holy Trinity, should recognize one universal and Catholic Church as Mother, whose commandments together with the ten of the law we should keep under pain of damnation, it is requisite that each one who aspires to eternal life should fix his eyes upon her. I, therefore, who am born of kings and relatives all baptized in her, as I myself also was, and what is more, from my infancy, unworthy as I am, have been called to the royal dignity, anointed and consecrated by the authority and by the ministers of the Church, under whose wing and in whose bosom I have been nourished and brought up, and by her instructed in the obedience due by all Christians to him whom she, guided by the Holy Spirit, has elected according to the ancient order and decrees of the primitive Church, to the holy Apostolic See as our head upon earth, to whom Jesus Christ in His last will has given power (speaking to St. Peter of her foundation on a living rock) of binding and loosing poor sinners from the chains of Satan, absolving us by himself or by his ministers for this purpose appointed, of all crimes or sins committed or perpetrated by us, we being repentant, as far as in us lies, making satisfaction for them after having confessed them according to the ordinance of the Church. I call my Saviour Jesus Christ to be my witness, the Blessed Trinity, the glorious Virgin Mary, all the Angels and Archangels, St. Peter, the pastor, my special intercessor and advocate, St. Paul, Apostle of the Gentiles, St. Andrew and all the holy apostles, St. George and in general all the Saints of Paradise,--that I have always lived in this faith, which is that of the universal Catholic Church, Apostolic and Roman, in which being regenerated, I have always had the intention of doing my duty to the holy Apostolic See. Of this, to my great regret, I have not been able to render due testimony to your Holiness, on account both of my detention in this captivity and of my long illness; but now that it has pleased God, my Holy Father, to permit for my sins and those of this unfortunate island, that I (the only one remaining of the blood of England and Scotland who makes profession of this faith) should, after twenty years of captivity, shut up in a narrow prison and at last condemned to die by the heretical States and Assembly of this country, as it has been to-day signified to me by the mouth of Lord Buckhurst, Amias Paulet my keeper, one Drew Drury, knight, and a secretary named Beale, in the name of their Queen, commanding me to prepare to receive death, offering me one of their bishops and a dean for my consolation (a priest that I had, having been taken from me long before by them, and held by them I know not where); I have thought it to be my first duty to turn me to God, and then to relate the whole to your Holiness in writing, to the end that, although I cannot let you hear it before my death, at least afterwards, the cause of it should be made manifest to you, which is, all things well considered and examined, their dread of subversion of their religion in this island, which they say I plan, and which is attempted for my sake, as well by those of their own subjects who obey your laws and are declared enemies (and who cause me to be prayed for as their Sovereign in their churches whose priests profess duty and subjection to me), as by strangers, and specially by the Catholic princes and my relations, and who (so they say) maintain my right to the crown of England. I leave it to your Holiness to consider the consequence of such a sentence, imploring you to have prayers made for my poor soul, and for all those who have died, or will die, in the same cause and the like sentence, and even in honour of God. I beg you to give your alms and incite the kings to do likewise to those who shall survive this shipwreck. And my intention being, according to the constitution of the Church, to confess, do penance as far as in me lies, and receive my Viaticum, if I can obtain my chaplain, or some other legitimate minister, to administer to me the said Sacraments; in default of this, with contrite and repentant heart, I prostrate myself at your Holiness' feet, confessing myself to God and to His Saints, and to the same your Paternity, as a very unworthy sinner and one meriting eternal damnation, unless it pleases the good God who died for sinners, to receive me in His infinite mercy among the number of poor penitent sinners trusting in his mercy--imploring you to take this my general confession in testimony of my intention to accomplish the remainder in the form ordained and commanded in the Church, if it is permitted me, and to give me your general absolution according as you know and think to be requisite for the glory of God, the honour of His Church, and the salvation of my poor soul, between which and the justice of God, I interpose the blood of Jesus Christ, crucified for me and all sinners, one of the most execrable among whom I confess myself to be, seeing the infinite grace I have received through Him, and which I have so little recognized and employed; the which would render me unworthy of forgiveness if His promise made to all those who, burdened with sin and spiritual woes coming to Him to be assisted by Him, and His mercy, did not encourage me, following His commandment to come to Him, bearing my burden in order to be relieved by Him of it like the prodigal son, and, what is more, offering my blood willingly at the foot of His cross, for the unwearied and faithful zeal which I bear to His Church, without the restoration of which I desire never to live in this unhappy world.

"And further, Holy Father, having left myself no goods in this world, I supplicate your Holiness to obtain from the very Christian king that my dowry should be charged with the payment of my debts, and the wages of my poor desolate servants, and with an annual obit for my soul and those of all our brethren departed in this just quarrel, having had no other private intention, as my poor servants, present at this, my affliction, will testify to you; as likewise how I have willingly offered my life in their heretical Assembly to maintain my Catholic, Apostolic and Roman religion, and to bring back those of this island who have ignorantly gone astray (to wit, themselves); protesting that in this case I would willingly deprive myself of all the title and dignity of a Queen, and do all honour and service to theirs, if she would cease to persecute the Catholics; as I protest that that is the end at which I have aimed since I have been in this country, and I have no ambition or desire to reign, nor to dispossess any other for my personal advantage, as by illness and by long afflictions I am so weakened that I have no longer any desire to trouble myself in this world except with the service of His Church, and to gain the souls of this island to God; in testimony of which, at my end, I do not wish to falter in preferring the public salvation to my personal interests of flesh and blood, which cause me to pray you,--with a mortal regret for the perdition of my poor child, after having tried by all means to regain him,--to be a true father to him, as St. John the Evangelist was to the youth whom he withdrew from the company of robbers; to take, in short, all the authority over him that I can give you to constrain him, and if it pleases you to call upon the Catholic king, to assist you in what touches temporal matters, and especially that you two may together try to ally him in marriage. And if God, for my sins, permit that he should remain obstinate, I knowing no Christian prince in these times who works so much for the faith, or who has so many means to aid him in the bringing back of this island, as the Catholic king, to whom I am much indebted and obliged, being the only one who aided me with his money and advice in my needs, I, subject to your good pleasure, leave him all that I can have of power or interest in the government of this kingdom if my son obstinately remains outside the Church. But if he finds he can bring him back, I desire he shall be aided, supported and advised by him (the king of Spain) and my relations of Guise, enjoining him by my last will to hold them, after you, as his fathers, and to ally himself by their advice and consent, or in one of their two houses. And if it pleased God, I would he were worthy to be a son of the Catholic king. This is the secret of my heart and the end of my desires in this world, tending as I mean them, to the good of His Church and to the discharge of my conscience, which I present at the feet of your Holiness, which I humbly kiss.

"You shall have the true account of the manner of my last taking, and all the proceedings against me, and by me, to the end that, hearing the truth, the calumnies which the enemies of the Church wish to lay upon me may be refuted by you and the truth known, and to this effect I have sent to you this bearer, requesting your holy blessing for the end, and saying to you for the last time *à Dieu*. Whom I pray in His grace to preserve your person for long, for the good of His Church and your sorrowful flock, especially that of this island, which I leave very much astray, without the mercy of God and without your paternal care.

"Fotheringay, 23rd November, 1586."

She adds a postscript and signs herself,

"Of your Holiness the very humble and devoted daughter

MARIE,

    Queen of Scotland,

    Dowager of France."

Her letter to Mendoça is written in a freer and clearer style, and is, I think, a truer picture of her thoughts, as they spontaneously form in her mind, than that to the Pope.

LETTER TO DON BERNARD DE MENDOÇA.

"My very dear Friend,--As I have always known you to be zealous in God's cause, and interested in my welfare and deliverance from captivity, I have likewise also always made you a sharer in all my intentions for the same cause, begging you to signify them to the king, Monsieur my good brother, for which at present, according to the little leisure I have, I have wished to send you this last adieu, being resolved to receive the death-stroke which was announced to me last Saturday.

"I know not when or in what manner, but at least you can feel assured and praise God for me that, by His grace, I had the courage to receive this very unjust sentence of the heretics with contentment for the honour which I esteem it to be to me to shed my blood at the demand of the enemies of His Church; whilst they honour me so much as to say that theirs cannot exist if I live; and the other point they affirm to be that their Queen cannot reign in security, for the same reason. In both these 'conditions' I, without contradicting them, accepted the honour they were so anxious to confer upon me, as very zealous in the Catholic religion, for which I had publicly offered my life; and as to the other matter, although I had made no attempt or taken any action to remove her who was in the place, still as they reproached me with what is my right, and is so considered by all Catholics, as they say, I did not wish to contradict them, leaving it to them to judge. But they, becoming angry in consequence of this, told me that, do what I would, I should not die for religion, but for having wished to have their Queen murdered, which I denied to them as being very false, as I never attempted anything of the kind, but left it to God and the Church to settle everything for this island regarding religion and what depends upon it.

"This bearer has promised me to relate to you how rigorously I have been treated by this people, and ill served by others, who I could wish had not so much shown their fear of death in so just a quarrel, or their inordinate passions. Whereas from me they only obtained the avowal that I was a free queen, Catholic, obedient to the Church, and that for my deliverance I was obliged--having tried for it by good means without being able to obtain it-- to procure it by the means which were offered to me, without approving (all the means employed).

"Nau has confessed all, Curle following his example, and all is thrown on me. They threaten me if I do not ask for pardon, but I say that, as they have already destined me to death, they may proceed in their injustice, hoping that God will recompense me in the other world. And through spite because I will not thus confess, they came the day before yesterday, Monday, to remove my dais, saying that I was no longer anything but a dead woman without any dignity.

"They are working in my hall; I think they are making a scaffold to make me play the last scene of the tragedy. I die in a good quarrel, and happy at having given up my rights to the king, your Master. I have said that if my son does not return to the bosom of the Church, I confess I know no princes more worthy or more suitable, for the protection of the island. I have written as much to His Holiness, and I beg you to certify to him that I die in this same wish, that I have written to you, and to him (you) know who is his near relative and old friend, and to a fourth who, above all others, I leave under the protection of the king, and require him, in the name of God, not to abandon them; and I beg them to serve him in my place. I cannot write to them. Salute them for me, and all of you pray God for my soul.

"I have asked for a priest, but do not know if I shall have one; they offered me one of their bishops. I utterly refused him. Believe what this bearer tells you, and these two poor women[#] who have been the nearest to me. They will tell you the truth. I beg of you to publish it, as I fear others will make it sound quite differently. Give orders that payment be made where you know of, for the discharge of my conscience; and may the churches of Spain keep me in remembrance in their prayers. Keep this bearer's secret; he has been a faithful valet to me.

[#] Jane Kennedy and Elizabeth Curle.

"May God give you a happy life. You will receive a token from me, of a diamond, which I valued as being that with which the late Duke of

Norfolk[#] pledged me his faith, and which I have nearly always worn. Keep it for love of me.

[#] Thomas Howard, Duke of Norfolk and Premier Peer of England, had been chairman of the Conference to which Mary's dispute with the rebels had been submitted in 1568. At that time, encouraged by many prominent members of the English nobility, he formed the design of marrying the Queen of Scots. He was betrayed to Elizabeth by the Regent Moray, to whom he had confided his plans. After a term of nine months in the Tower, he was set at liberty. Resuming negotiations with Mary and her friends, he was again betrayed--this time by his secretary--and being convicted of treasonable practices, was put to death.

"I do not know if I shall be allowed to make a will. I have asked for leave, but they have all my money. God be with you. Forgive me if I write with pain and trouble, having not even one solitary person to aid me or make my rough copies and to write from my dictation. If you cannot read my handwriting this bearer will read it to you, or my Ambassador, who is familiar with it. Among other accusations, Criton's is one about which I know nothing. I fear much that Nau and Pasquier have much hastened my death, for they kept some papers, and also they are people who wish to live in both worlds, if they can have their commodities. I would to God that Fontenay had been here; he is a young man of strong resolution and knowledge. Adieu.

"Once more I recommend to you my poor destitute servants, and beg you to pray for my soul.

"From Fotheringay, this Wednesday, the 23rd of November. I recommend to you the poor Bishop of Ross, who will be quite destitute.

"Your much obliged and perfect friend.

MARIE R."

The Duke of Guise being nearly related to her, would be expected to regard the treatment which she received as something personally touching himself and his family. Wishing, therefore, to inspire him with the thoughts that sustained her own spirits when, as she was convinced, the gates of martyrdom were opening to receive her into a better world, she penned him the following spirited letter:--

"From Fotheringay, the 24th of November,

"My Good Cousin:--You whom I hold as dearest to me in the world, being ready through unjust judgment, to be put to a death such as no one of our race, thanks be to God, has ever suffered, still less one of my quality; but my good cousin, praise God for it, as I was useless in the world, for the cause of God and His Church in the state I was, and I hope my death will testify to my constancy in the faith, and my readiness to die for the upholding and restoration of the Church in this unhappy island. And, although no executioner has ever before dipped his hand in our blood, be not ashamed of it my dear friend, for the condemnation of heretics and enemies of the Church (and who have no jurisdiction over me, a free queen) is profitable before God for the children of His Church. If I would belong to them I should not receive this blow. All those of our house have been persecuted by this sect; for example, your good father, with whom I hope to be received by the mercy of the just Judge. I recommend to you, then, my poor servants, the discharge of my debts, and I beg you to have some annual obit founded for my soul, not at your expense, but please make the necessary solicitations and give the orders which shall be required. And you shall understand my intention by these, my poor desolate servants, eye-witnesses of my last tragedy.

"May God prosper you, your wife, children, brothers and cousins, and above all our chief, my good brother and cousin, and all his. May the blessing of God and that which I would give to children of my own, be on yours, whom I recommend no less to God than my own unfortunate and ill-advised child.

"You will receive some token from me, to remind you to pray for the soul of your poor cousin, destitute of all aid and advice but that of God, which gives me strength and courage to resist alone so many wolves howling after me. To God be the glory.

"Believe, in particular, all that shall be said to you by a person who will give you a ruby ring from me, for I take it upon my conscience that the truth shall be told you of what I have charged her with, especially of what touches my poor servants, and regarding one of them in particular. I recommend you this person on account of her straightforward sincerity and goodness, and so that she may be placed in some good situation. I have chosen her as being most impartial and the one who will the most simply convey my orders. I beg of you not to make it known that she has said anything to you in private, as envy might harm her.

"I have suffered much for two years or more, and could not let you know it for important reasons, God be praised for all, and may He give you the grace to persevere in the service of His Church as long as you live, and may this honour never leave our race; so that we, men as well as women, may be ready to shed our blood to maintain the quarrel of the faith, putting aside all worldly interests. And as for me, I esteem myself born, both on the paternal and maternal side, to offer my blood for it, and I have no intention of degenerating. May Jesus, for us crucified, and may all the holy martyrs by their intercession, render us worthy of willingly offering our bodies to His Glory.

"Thinking to degrade me, they had my dais taken down, and afterwards my guardian came to offer to write to their Queen, saying he had not done this by her order, but by the advice of some of the council. I showed them the cross of my Saviour in the place where my arms had been on the said dais. You shall hear of our conversation. They have been more gentle since.

"Your affectionate cousin and perfect friend,

MARIE,

      Queen of Scotland,

      Dowager of France."

CHAPTER XV.

AN INTERVAL OF SUSPENSE.

The end did not come so quickly as Mary had expected. Although the sentence had been publicly proclaimed throughout the kingdom, Elizabeth hesitated to sign the death-warrant. She saw that the execution of the Scottish queen might be fraught with dangerous consequences to herself and the realm, and it was not her policy to make a perilous advance without having provided the means for a safe retreat. If she could only find some servant who, "upon the winking of authority could understand a law," her purpose would be better served. Mary would be secretly removed, and a scapegoat would be at hand to bear the sin, and, if needs be, the punishment due to it. On February the 1st, she signed the death-warrant, which had been placed before her among a number of other papers, and impressed upon Assistant Secretary Davison that she did not wish to be troubled further with that matter. Indeed she continued to complain of the lack of zeal in those who had joined the Association for her defence. She had done all, she said, that could be required of her by law or reason, and those who were interested in her welfare should relieve her of further responsibility. "Would it not be better for me," she remarked, "to risk personal danger than to take the life of a relation. But if a loyal subject were to save me from the embarrassment of dealing the blow, the resentment of Scotland and France might be disarmed." The prudence of those "loyal subjects" who preferred to leave the responsibility on her own shoulders, was amply vindicated immediately after the execution, when, in the futile endeavour to deceive the French and Spanish ambassadors, she visited Burleigh and other Ministers with temporary suspension from office, and cast Davison into the Tower, where she left him to languish for the remainder of her lifetime, because forsooth they had executed the death-warrant without her knowledge. Walsingham and Davison felt constrained, however, to write Sir Amias Paulet and Sir Drew Drury, whom the Queen thought should be ready to do her will, to point out to them the service their royal Mistress expected from them. "We find," they wrote, "by speech lately uttered by Her Majesty that she doth note in you a lack of that care and zeal of her service that she looked for at your hands, in that you have not in all this time of yourselves (without other provocation) found out some way to shorten the life of the Queen, considering the great peril she (Elizabeth) is subject unto hourly, so long as the said Queen shall live........

"And therefore she (Elizabeth) taketh it most unkindly towards her, that men professing that love towards her that you do, should in any kind or sort, for lack of the discharge of your duties, cast the burthen upon her, knowing, as you do, her indisposition to shed blood, especially of one of that sex and quality, and so near to her in blood as the said Queen is." Closing, they commit Paulet and Drury "to the *protection* of the Almighty"--which was very thoughtful, seeing how persuasively they had just been soliciting them to an act of assassination. Paulet, in spite of his fierce hatred of Mary, unequivocally refused to entertain the suggestion and expressed his regret that he had lived to see the unhappy day in which he was "required by direction from her most gracious sovereign, to do an act which God and the law forbiddeth." Then, with exquisite propriety of terminology, he commits Walsingham and Davison, not to the "*protection*"--the time when they most needed protection he probably thought was past--but to "the *mercy* of the Almighty."

In the meantime the preparations for the execution were advancing. Elizabeth having signed the death-warrant, Davison handed it over to the Chancellor; at the instance of the Lord Treasurer, Burleigh, the Council convened, and, without waiting further instructions from the Queen, appointed the Earls of Kent and Shrewsbury to execute the warrant.

While her fate was being sealed at Westminster, the doomed captive in Fotheringay was expecting, from day to day, to receive the final blow. Though frequently confined to bed by rheumatism in her limbs, she maintained a cheerfulness and composure that greatly annoyed the irascible Paulet. On December the 15th, he complains to Walsingham that "this lady continues to show her perverse and obstinate character." "She shows," he adds, "no sign of repentance and no submission. She does not acknowledge her fault, does not ask for forgiveness and shows no sign of wishing to live."

On the 19th of December, she penned a letter of which the following is a portion, to Queen Elizabeth:--

"Madame, in honour of Jesus (whose name all powers obey), I require you to promise that when my enemies shall have satisfied their dark desire for my innocent blood, you will permit that my poor sorrowful servants may altogether bear my body to be buried in holy ground and near those of my predecessors who are in France, especially the late queen, my mother; and this because in Scotland the bodies of the kings, my ancestors, have been insulted, and the churches pulled down and profaned, and because, suffering death in this country, I cannot have a place beside your predecessors, who are also mine; and what is more important, because in our religion we must prize being buried in holy ground. And as I am told you wish in nothing to force my conscience or my religion, and have even conceded me a priest, I hope that you will not refuse this my last request, but will at least allow free sepulture to the body from which the soul will be separated, as being united, they never knew how to obtain liberty to live in peace, or to procure the same for you, for which before God I do not in any way blame you--but may God show you the entire truth after my death.

"And because I fear the secret tyranny of some of those into whose power you have abandoned me, I beg you not to permit me to be executed without your knowledge--not from fear of the pain, which I am ready to suffer, but on account of the rumours which would be spread concerning my death if it was not seen by reliable witnesses; how it was done, I am persuaded, in the case of others of different rank. It is for this reason that in another place I require that my attendants remain to be spectators and witnesses of my end in the faith of my Saviour, and in the obedience of His Church, and afterwards they shall all together quickly withdraw, taking my body with them as secretly as you wish, and so that the furniture and other things which I may be able to leave them in dying, be not taken from them, which will be, indeed a very small reward for their good service. Would you wish me to return a jewel, which you gave me, to you with my last words, or would it please you to receive it sooner? I implore of you anew to permit me to send a jewel and a last adieu to my son, together with my blessing, of which he has been deprived, owing to that you informed me of his refusal to enter into a treaty in which I was included,--by the unhappy advice of whom? The last point I leave to your conscience and favourable consideration. For the others I demand of you, in the name of Jesus Christ, and in consideration of our relationship, in remembrance of King Henry VII., your grandfather and mine[#] and in honour of the dignity we have both held, and of our common sex, that my request be granted.

[#] Henry VII. was Elizabeth's grandfather and Mary's great-grandfather.

"For the rest I think you will certainly have heard that they pulled down my dais, by your order, as they said, and that afterwards they told me that it was not done by your command but by that of some of the Council. I praise God that such cruelty, which could only show malice and affect me after I had made up my mind to die, came not from you. I fear it has been like this in many other things, and that this is the reason why they would not permit me to write to you until they had, as far as they could, taken from me all external mark of dignity and power, telling me I was simply a dead woman, stripped of all dignity.

"God be praised for all. I wish that all my papers, without any exception, had been shown to you, so that it might have been said that it was not solely the care of your safety which animated all those who are so prompt in pursuing me. If you grant me this, my last request, give orders that I shall see what you write regarding it, as otherwise they will make me believe what they like; and I desire to know your final reply to my final request.

"In conclusion, I pray the God of mercy, the just Judge, that He will deign to enlighten you by His Holy Spirit, and that He will give me the grace to die in perfect charity, as I am preparing myself to do, pardoning all those who are the cause of my death, or who have co-operated in it, and this shall be my prayer till the end. I consider it happy for me that it should come before the persecution which I foresee threatens this island--if God is not more truly feared and revered, and vanity and worldly policy not more wisely curbed. Do not accuse me of presumption if, on the eve of leaving this world, and preparing myself for a better, I remind you that one day you will have to answer for your charge as well as those who are sent before, and that, making no account of my blood or my country, I desire to think of the time when, from the earliest dawn of reason, we were taught to place our soul's welfare before all temporal matters, which should cede to those of eternity.

"Your Sister and Cousin wrongfully imprisoned,

MARIE, QUEEN."

She wrote again to Elizabeth nearly a month later, but Paulet refused to dispatch her letter.

CHAPTER XVI.

THE END.

What lovely form, in deepest gloom

Of prison cave, awaits her doom?--

* * * * *

'Tis Scotia's basely-injured Queen;

'Tis she who, cherished, would have been

The loveliest, brightest, richest gem

In Caledonia's diadem,--

A gem too polished, pure and bright

For Scotia's sons, in Scotia's night,

When evil man and evil times

Were stained in basest, blackest crimes.--

The Royal Exile.

On Tuesday, the 7th of February (1587), the Earls of Kent and Shrewsbury, who had been appointed to conduct the execution of the Scottish queen, arrived at Fotheringay. Towards evening they sent her word that they wished to see her on urgent business. She had gone to bed, but, on hearing their message, she rose and prepared to receive them. Shrewsbury and Kent entered, accompanied by Beale, clerk of the Council, and the two keepers, Paulet and Drury. Shrewsbury, who in his heart sympathized with the helpless queen, performed the unpleasant duty imposed upon him by announcing to her the purpose of their visit, and requesting her to listen to the sentence which Beale was about to read. When Beale had finished reading, Mary thanked them for the welcome news. "I have long looked for this," she said, "and have expected it day by day for eighteen years. Unworthy though I think myself, I am by the grace of God a Queen born and a Queen anointed, a near relative of the Queen (of England), grand-daughter of King Henry VII., and I have had the honour to be Queen of France, but, in all my life I have had only sorrow." In answer to their urgent requests that she should accept of the religious services of the Dean of Peterborough, and renounce her former "abominations," she assured them that all their efforts to persuade her in that matter were useless. "Having lived till now in the true faith," she said, "this is not the time to change, but on the contrary, it is the very moment when it is most needful that I should remain firm and constant, as I intend to do." Turning from the profitless religious discussion on which Kent seemed disposed to linger, she enquired when she should die. "To-morrow morning at eight o'clock," was Shrewsbury's reply.

Short indeed was the notice, but Mary betrayed no sign of alarm. The lords shortly after retired, and she was left alone to prepare for the closing scene in the painful tragedy of her life. She was denied the assistance of a priest--a last act of cruelty for which no excuse can be offered.

The little family of her faithful servants who had shared with her the weary years of captivity, were disconsolate. She alone was bright and joyful. "Well," she said, "let supper be hastened, so that I may put my affairs in order. My children, it is now no time to weep; that is useless; what do you now fear? You should rather rejoice to see me on such a good road to being delivered from the many evils and afflictions which have so long been my portion." During supper she turned to her physician, Bourgoin, with a bright countenance, and said:--"Did you remark what Lord Kent said in his interview with me? He said that my life would have been the death of their religion, and that my death will be its life. Oh, how happy these words make me............ They told me that I was to die because I had plotted against the Queen, and here is Lord Kent sent to me to convert me, and what does he tell me?--that I am to die on account of my religion."

When the light repast was finished, her attendants gathered around her on their knees, implored her to forgive them whatever offences they had committed against her. "With all my heart, my children," she fervently answered, "even as I pray you to forgive me any injustice or harshness of which I may have been guilty towards you."

Her unselfishness, which was one of the strongest features of her character, showed itself to the last. No one would have thought it was she who had to die next morning. She was administering comfort, not seeking it. In all her life she had never abandoned a friend, nor forgotten a good turn; nor did she now. The night was already well advanced, and she began parcelling out gifts of money and jewellery for her attendants and friends. Late in the night she wrote a short letter to her chaplain, Preau, who was detained in another part of the Castle and denied admittance to her presence.

"I have," she wrote, "been attacked to-day concerning my religion, and urged to receive consolation from the heretics. You will hear from Bourgoin and others that I, at least, faithfully made protestation for my faith, in which I wish to die. I requested to have you, in order that I might make my confession and receive my Sacrament, which was cruelly refused me, as well as leave for my body to be removed and the power of making a free will, or writing anything except what shall pass through their hands and be subject to the good pleasure of their mistress. In default of that, I confess in general the gravity of my sins, as I had intended to do to you in particular, begging you in the name of God to pray and watch with me this night in satisfaction for my sins, and to send me your absolution and pardon for the things in which I have offended you. I shall try to see you in their presence, as they have allowed me to see the steward,[#] and if I am allowed, I shall ask the blessing on my knees before all.

[#] Melville, the steward here referred to, and Preau had been separated from Mary three weeks before. Melville was permitted to meet his mistress on her way to the scaffold. Preau was denied even this.

"Advise me as to the most appropriate prayers, for this night and to-morrow morning, as the time is short and I have no leisure to write; but I will recommend you, as well as the others, and especially your benefices will be spared to you, and I will recommend you to the king. I have no more time. Tell me in writing of all that you shall think best for the good of my soul. I shall send you a last little token."

"At two hours after midnight," she wrote a letter to the King of France, and then, worn out with the anxieties and labours of the last twelve hours, laid down to rest. But her women attendants, who watched closely by her bedside, assure us that, though she lay calm and motionless with her hands crossed on her breast, her lips continued to move in prayer, and a joyful expression occasionally rested on her countenance.

The royal victim rose early in the morning, and attired herself in her most costly garments.[#] Then she called together her little household, gave to each the present she had prepared the night before, and with comforting words bade them farewell. "I beg you all," she said, "to assist at my death, and to testify to my unalterable devotion to my religion. Be ye witnesses of my last acts and my last words." This done, she retired to her oratory to pray. At eight o'clock the sheriff interrupted her devotions, announcing that the hour had come. The Queen promptly answered the summons, and, although suffering from a rheumatism which prevented her from walking without support, she strove to disguise her suffering and to march to death with as firm a step as possible. At the foot of the stairs leading down from her apartments, her old servant Melville awaited his mistress, and, on her approach, threw himself on his knees before her, and wept. "Ah, madame," he said, "unhappy me, what man on earth was ever before the messenger of so important sorrow and heaviness as I shall be, when I shall report that my good and gracious Queen and Mistress is beheaded in England."

[#] "Her robes--the only ones she had reserved of former splendours--were such as were then worn by queens-dowager. The skirt and bodice of black satin were worn over a petticoat of russet-brown velvet; while the long regal mantle, also of black satin, embroidered with gold and trimmed with fur, had long hanging sleeves and a train. The Queen's head-dress was of white crape, from which fell a long veil of the same delicate material, edged with lace. Round her neck she wore a chain of scented beads with a cross, and at her waist a golden rosary." (*The Tragedy of Fotheringay*, by Hon. Mrs. Maxwell Scott.)

"Not so," replied the Queen; "to-day, good Melville, thou seest the end of Mary Stewart's miseries, that should rejoice thee. Thou knowest that this world is but vanity and misery. Be the bearer of this news, that I die a Catholic, firm in my religion, a faithful Scotchwoman and a true Frenchwoman. God forgive those who have sought my death." She advanced unmoved through the hall in which the scaffold stood, carrying in her uplifted hand a large ivory crucifix. After encountering much opposition, she succeeded in obtaining permission for her two women, Jane Kennedy and Elizabeth Curle, to assist her until she should be disrobed for the execution.

Having mounted the scaffold, she seated herself on a low stool covered with black, while the warrant of execution was being read. When it was finished, she signed herself with the sign of the Cross and (as an eye witness says), "She looked upon the assembly with a joyous countenance, her beauty more apparent than ever, a bright colour in her face." Mr. Fletcher, Dean of Peterborough, then approached the scaffold railing and began to address her. But she paid no heed to him, except to inform him that he need not trouble himself further, for she was settled in her religion. On the contrary, as if indifferent to what was being said and done around her, she glided from the stool on which she sat, and kneeling down prayed aloud for the afflicted Church of Christ, for her son, for Queen Elizabeth, "that she might prosper and serve God aright," for her enemies who had long sought her blood; finally, kissing the crucifix, which she held in her hand, she begged that Jesus, whose arms were there extended on the cross, would receive her into the arms of his mercy. Her prayer ended, the executioners began to disrobe her. At this point her women, no longer able to control their feelings, broke into lamentations, but she embracing them, prayed them not to cry, or she would be obliged to send them away. Turning to where her men-servants stood, a short distance from the scaffold, she crossed them with her hands and bade them farewell.

All being now ready, she embraced her women, saying, "Adieu for the last time,--Adieu, au revoir," and then requested them to withdraw from the scaffold.

Seated on the black stool, her eyes bandaged, and the crucifix raised in her hands, she prays aloud, "My God, I have hoped in thee, I give back my soul into Thy hands." The executioners lead her to the block; Lord Shrewsbury lifts up his wand; a deep silence falls upon the hall as the axe trembles in the air, and is broken only by the last words of Mary Stewart as she awaits the deadly blow,--"Into Thy hands, O Lord, I commend my spirit."

"The neck is bared--the blow is struck--the soul is passed away,

The bright, the beautiful, is now--a bleeding piece of clay."

The executioner taking up the head, according to custom, and exposing it to the gaze of the people, cried out, "God save the Queen." "So perish all the Queen's enemies," added the Dean of Peterborough; "such be the end of all the Queen's and the Gospel's enemies," remarked the Earl of Kent. But even that hostile assembly was melted to tears, and scarcely a voice was heard to answer, "Amen."

The body of the Scottish Queen, notwithstanding her dying request that it be consigned to the care of her servants and by them borne away to France and laid beside that of her mother, was detained for six months in Fotheringay Castle. It was then removed, by order of Elizabeth, to the Cathedral of Peterborough, a few miles distant, and laid in a vault opposite the tomb of another noble victim of Tudor tyranny, the blameless Catherine of Arragon. Twenty-five years later her son, King James, who had in the meantime succeeded to the throne of England, in partial reparation for his former neglects, removed her remains to Westminster Abbey, and caused a beautiful monument, with a marble effigy of the Queen in a recumbent position, to be erected over them, in the south aisle of Henry the Seventh's chapel.

No more need be added to this brief review of Mary Stewart's history. The opinions set forth and defended in the above pages will not be received by all, for the leading events of her life will continue to be interpreted very generally according to theories conceived by party zeal, before the historical evidence bearing on them has been examined. I do not pretend that I myself have approached the study of her life without prejudice. Say what we will, where party spirit has run high, our feelings are always enlisted before our judgment has been moved. This, however, should be borne in mind: the prejudices of a writer cannot destroy the force of the evidence with which he supports his contention; and, whithersoever my sympathies may tend, I have endeavoured to give my reasons--the intelligent reader will judge of their value--why I refuse to believe that Mary was the paramour of Bothwell and a party to the murder of her husband, and why I maintain that her conviction, on the charge of having sanctioned the projected murder of Queen Elizabeth, was unjust.